MW01634342

IN BETWEEN

Also edited by Miriam Hodgson

Love Hurts

Mother's Day

for younger readers

Prima Ballerina

IN BETWEEN

Stories of Leaving Childhood

EDITED BY
MIRIAM HODGSON

Methuen Children's Books

First published in Great Britain 1994
by Methuen Children's Books
a imprint of Reed Consumer Books Limited
Michelin House, 81 Fulham Road, London SW3 6RB
and Auckland, Melbourne, Singapore and Toronto

ISBN 0 416 19064 2

A CIP catalogue record for this book is
available at the British Library

Printed in England by Clays Ltd, St Ives plc

Contents

*For Elke Lacey, best of colleagues, best of friends.
She grew up but did not grow old.*

Foreword

It was Elke Lacey in one of our daily chats before the office day officially began who gave me the idea of this anthology. We talked about the moment you think you've grown up, that stage when you seem to be in between childhood and adulthood. Graham Greene's phrase in *The Power and the Glory* seems to sum it up perfectly: 'There is always one moment in childhood when the door opens and lets the future in.' Is it when you first fall in love? Is it when you realise it is you who can control what happens in your life? Is it when you realise you can't hide behind anyone else except yourself as in Elizabeth Laird's *The Scream*?

Is it when circumstances blast you out of childhood as in Michael Morpurgo's terrifying *What Does It Feel Like??* or Joanna Carey's sobering *Down to Earth* where the girl has never had a childhood?

Is it when you decide no one is going to tell you what to think any more as in Vivien Alcock's *Cinderella Girl*? Is it when you consciously revert to childhood, backing away from an adult situation, but behave in an adult way as in Jacqueline Wilson's *The Favourite*?

Is it when you are at the right age at the wrong time as in Sam McBratney's *SWALK*?

Is it when you realise that you must face loss and pain at some time as in Adèle Geras's *The Mahdi Sisters*?

Is it when you are caught in a struggle between fantasy and reality as in Alick Rowe's *The Facts of Life*?

Growing up can be when you can accept and like the fact that people are not what you first thought they were as in Rachel Anderson's *Roz and the Smiling Knee*. Or when you leap over an imaginery barrier and a friend who has known you only as a child cannot follow you as in Ian Strachan's *The Simple Truth*.

Above all is growing up when you no longer feel 'safe in the realms of childhood' as in Robert Westall's *The Women's Hour*?

What is common to all of the stories is their faithfulness to the intensity of feelings that being in between childhood and adulthood brings. What emerges is a reminder that the frontier between childhood and adulthood is never closed. Are we ever not in between?

SWALK

SAM McBRATNEY

The card he was expecting arrived a day early. Monty Quayle found it waiting for him when he got home from school on the thirteenth of February. His first impulse was to chuck it on the fire there and then and be done with it, for he had no time for this slushy, lovey-dovey St Valentine's Day nonsense; but he didn't do that. Perhaps the sheer size of the white envelope appealed to his sense of curiosity. It seemed a good deal too large for his letterbox.

'Who's your admirer, then?' his mother asked slyly as she passed through the kitchen trailing coffee fumes.

'Some twit of a girl,' he said.

'In your form?'

'How do I know?' said Monty, heading smartly for the privacy of his own room. His mother had had two questions and two answers on this subject – more than she had a right to expect.

Actually he had a pretty good idea who was torturing him in this way. In yesterday's French class Gail Summers and Anne Clarke had informed him that he would be receiving a valentine card on February the fourteenth.

'How do you know?' he'd asked in all innocence.

'A wee bird told us,' they said, adding that this

card would have the French word for 'love' on it. 'L'amour,' they said, and started to laugh until Anne Clarke sounded like a camel.

In the peace and quiet of his own room Monty examined the uninvited card with as much generosity of spirit as he could muster. One of the giant red hearts on the front had a jagged split running through it, and it sickened him, that broken heart. Your heart was a thumping big muscle in the middle of your chest, it couldn't snap in two like a cheese and onion crisp and how people could ignore a simple fact like that was beyond his understanding. 'My heart longs for you,' said one of the lines inside. Hearts couldn't long for anything, they were for pumping blood and you might as well long for somebody with your left kidney. 'My brain longs for you' would be better. Not that he wanted Gail Summers' or Anne Clarke's brain to long for him either, but at least it would make sense from a biological point of view.

The whole card was a mass of scrawled verses which were so awful that he couldn't stop reading them. What could one say about:

'Roses are red,
Violets are blue,
If I had three feet,
You'd be my third shoe'?

A long stick of French bread had been drawn in one corner with a beret on its head. It also had legs. And sunglasses. 'L'amour,' said the heart-shaped bubble escaping from the mouth of this loaf.

Those two were the guilty ones, all right.

On the reverse side of the envelope Monty noticed a word he had never seen before. It didn't even look English. SWALK. What did that mean?

Was it yet more French? Monty shoved the whole lot between the pages of an atlas.

Overnight the snow came down. The cars on every road took their time that morning. Although the pavements were awash with melting slush, you could still find the makings of a snowball on the tops of walls or lying on a hedge, and Monty found himself attacked by two people as he approached the school gates. Like most of the girls he knew, those two couldn't throw a snowball to save their lives.

'You missed,' he said.

'Did you get a valentine card this morning?' shouted Anne Clarke, snorting out steam like a dragon.

'No I didn't, hard cheese.'

'Well, we know somebody who sent you one, don't we, Gail?'

'Did you send it?'

'Us?' Anne Clarke released a howl and a giggle into the morning air. 'What makes you think it was *us*?'

Monty did not understand this behaviour, so he went into school hoping that his friend Conor would be back after his dose of the flu.

During the morning he made a point of standing at the back of every line, a tactic which allowed him to go into each classroom last and so avoid Anne Clarke and Gail Summers. If he went in first, they might sit down beside him. Conor couldn't understand why he wasn't pushing and shoving for a radiator seat like everybody else.

In French he put up his hand and asked, quietly, 'Miss Peters, is SWALK a French word?'

She peered at him through the rainbow-framed glasses on the bridge of her nose. She didn't have to peer far, for Monty had been forced to take a seat at the front of the room. Under her nose, in fact.

'What?'

'SWALK, Miss, is it French?'

'Spell it.'

'S–W–A–L–K.'

Some tittering behind made him wonder whether he had asked an intelligent question.

'Are you trying to be funny, Monty Quayle?' said Miss Peters icily, then went on to describe the peculiar habits of some French verb, leaving unsolved the mystery of SWALK.

According to a powerful rumour which invaded the school at lunchtime, all the teachers were afraid of being snowed in and the place was closing early; but that didn't happen. As Conor and Monty walked home at the usual time, Conor – imitating Miss Peters – said, 'Are you trying to be funny, Monty Quayle!' Millions of his flu germs were spluttered over the slushy grey snow. 'I nearly wet myself when you asked her about SWALK.'

And Monty smiled, as if thinking up such humorous things came naturally to him.

'You didn't get a valentine card?' Conor asked shrewdly – a little dart of a question.

'You must be kidding,' said Monty. 'Me? Valentine cards?'

When he got home it was to find that a second card had been delivered to his house, by hand, without a stamp, simply pushed through his front door without so much as a by-your-leave. Monty saw no reason why that sort of thing should be legal.

'Is it from the same person?' his mother wanted to know as she hovered there.

'I don't know,' said Monty, staring at the two

words written in capitals on the flap. SWALK and SWALK. Two of them. Plural swalks.

'What does SWALK actually mean?' he asked, making use of his mother.

'Sealed with a loving kiss.'

'Cut out the goo talk, Mum!'

'It does. Goo talk, indeed! S for sealed, W for with, L for loving, K for kiss. It's short for "sealed with a loving kiss".'

Hell's bells! And he'd asked Miss Peters, who now thought of him as a fool, if it was French – she'd think he was girl-mad. Sealed with a loving kiss! Oh, the shame of it, and he hated kissing; his relatives no longer tried it on because he'd put a stop to it – on TV he hated that cissy lip stuff and the horrible sucking noises made by people joined together at their mouths! The humiliation he felt was colossal – his pride all drained away.

He threw the valentine card on the fire and watched until both SWALKs were consumed by it utterly.

'Well, that's not a very nice way to get on,' his mother said. Not that he cared. She had no understanding of the situation whatsoever.

I'll send *them* a card! Monty raved upstairs. I'll send them some card, all right, and it'll be plastered with words the French never heard of. SWAFEJ, he thought. Sealed with a frog's eyeball juice. And SWAMS. Sealed with a monkey's stink. In no time at all he had over a dozen good ones – letters sealed with acid rain, elephant's wee-wee, a pelican's egg yolk, lubricating oil, mashed maggots and worse. Much worse. This line of thinking was effective in its own way, for he had calmed down quite a lot by the time he looked out of his bedroom window and saw both of them standing in the street below.

They had a spaniel-looking dog lolloping round their legs. The sight of this thing's floppy ears and its big soft belly as round as a melon inspired Monty with a cunning idea. Down the stairs he flew three at a time, calling out for Mighty Wolf to appear by his side.

Their yappy mongrel had actually been named Patch for an obvious reason, but he also answered to names like Fleabag, Lagerlout and Mighty Wolf. That dog hated every living thing that did not belong to his own family; and it hated, besides, non-living things within the family. (The hoover was its mortal enemy.) If you held up a mirror he also went beserk, which meant that Mighty Wolf was a creature who even hated himself. Monty opened the front door just enough – and let him loose. Some people were about to learn that it didn't pay to lurk.

This plan backfired horribly, as Monty had to admit when he sneaked down the path some moments later. His fool of a dog was actually showing off in front of the spaniel with a display of athletic twirls and frisky jumps. In between the twirls and jumps there occurred some rubbing of noses. SWALK, thought Monty – bitterly – again. It was as if the creature knew it was St Valentine's Day.

'Your dog likes Sheila,' said Anne Clark.

'He's just friendly,' lied Monty, scooping up the animal into his arms. This was to stop the disgusting smelling of behinds that was now going on.

'Did you get a valentine card?'

'Yes I did.' He was flustered, and could not duck the question.

'We know who sent it even though there's no

name on it, don't we, Gail?'

Gail Summers blushed until her cheeks glowed; and then the beast within the cradle of Monty's arms began to whine with desire. A stump of a tail flicked backwards and forwards in front of his face like a windscreen wiper.

'It wants its tea,' Monty explained, retreating smartly up the path and into the house again, where Mighty Wolf got told in no uncertain terms what a big soft wet pudding he had degenerated into.

About the same time on the following day there came a knock at the front door which Monty, to his regret, left for his mother to answer.

She returned saying, 'It's young Gail Summers. She wants to know: is your dog coming out? And you needn't look at me like that – go and speak to her.'

There she stood on his step, with spaniel, wearing a woollen hat and a scarf that seemed to go round her neck at least three times. Not much of her face could be seen, actually.

'Is Patch coming out?' she asked.

Patch, he thought. And how did she get to know Fleabag's real name? No doubt enquiries had been made.

'He's got a thorn in his foot.'

'Is it sore?'

'We had to bathe it.'

'Did you use hot water?'

'And disinfectant,' Monty assured her, while holding on to the door in case Mighty Wolf put in an appearance.

'Well, bye-bye, then,' said Gail, with a twist at Sheila Spaniel's lead, 'I'll see you in school tomorrow.'

'Goodbye,' said Monty, as if he was leaving that night for Australia.

This business about the valentine cards forced him to take a look at himself in the long mirror that evening, and to ask: what could there be about that person on the other side of the looking glass to drive someone to send him a card that was sealed, not once, but twice, with a loving kiss? Surely such magnetism in a human being would be recognisable? All the same, he couldn't find it. After viewing himself from many angles he remained none the wiser.

Going to school next day he noticed Gail Summers on the road ahead of him. Now it was certainly a treacherous morning for walking, and ridges of frozen slush glittered in the early sunlight; but he knew fine rightly that she was not walking slowly because of the ice. The idea was that he should catch up with her, which he did.

'Daddy had to break the ice on our pond this morning,' she said.

'Goldfish?' he said.

'No. It's for wildlife. Goldfish eat tadpoles. One slurp and they're gone.'

'My girlfriend has goldfish,' Monty suddenly blurted out. 'They're big ones as long as your foot, I'd say.'

'Who is she?'

The sheer cheek of this question — the colossal amount of nosiness involved in it — allowed Monty to glare at her angrily.

'It's none of your business who she is.'

'You haven't got one, that's why.'

'That's where you're wrong.'

'Well, who is she, then?'

She didn't believe him! In spite of the fact that

he'd even described his girlfriend's goldfish, his word on this important subject was not good enough for her!

'She's Glenda Finch, if you must know.'

Glenda was a rough sort, the sort who pulled hair and who wouldn't take kindly to someone who tried to steal her boyfriend. On the spur of the moment she was a very good choice, Monty was thinking. As he parted company with Gail Summers he felt that he had solved his problem, for anybody with any sense would now find another person to pursue.

At breaktime Conor told him that Glenda Finch was looking for him.

'What for?'

'Dunno,' said Conor. 'Something to do with rumours and goldfish. She says you're saying things about her and she's going to squash you like a grub. You know what she's like.'

Oh God. Only too well, he knew what Glenda was like. No matter which point of the compass she approached from you heard her coming, and you heard her go. She went through life making mountains out of molehills and molehills out of mountains.

Rather like a mole himself, Monty went underground for the rest of the morning. Great care had to be taken while crossing the playground, and he longed for a periscope to enable him to see round corners and down corridors. Often he reflected on the treachery of girls like Gail Summers, who could send you a letter sealed with a loving kiss on a Tuesday and then land you right in it the day after.

At lunchtime Glenda Finch trapped him in the crowded room where people went to eat their sandwiches. There was, in fact, an open window hand, but only a genuine coward could have done a bunk like that.

'You're saying things about me, Monty Quayle! You said I'm your *girlfriend*!'

The whole situation – he saw as one detached – was just completely crazy. And the craziest thing of all was that, yes, somehow he *had* said that. My girlfriend is Glenda Finch, he'd said. And why? He must have been temporarily insane. Glenda could never be anyone's girlfriend, for crying out loud, it would be too dangerous.

'And you said I sent you a valentine card! You'd better watch it, Quayle. I wouldn't send you a valentine card for a pension and I wouldn't be your girlfriend if you were the last person left alive after a nuclear bomb. And I haven't got *goldfish*!' she screamed, finishing on a high note. Monty wondered desperately if he could pretend that there was another Glenda Finch.

There was more. Monty fought back with such statements as 'Shut your spout, fat whale,' in order to avoid being overwhelmed completely. After the contest he felt quite tingly and invigorated – as joggers must do, he reflected.

And Gail Summers did not trouble him from that time on.

The days raced by, and the long evenings of summer came again. That was the year when the Quayle family went abroad for the first time on a camping holiday in Northern France. Part of the thinking behind the holiday was that Monty would get a chance to practise his French, but he spent the time playing with English-speaking children and got by with a few French words for sweets. While they were away Mighty Wolf attacked a moving

Volkswagen in the street and banjoed his leg. The mutt recovered all right, but once arthritis set into his left hip he could hardly muster the enthusiasm to see off a stray cat.

Two more summers went by. Monty found himself looking up at the sky at night, and wondered about the distances between the stars – a thing he had never done before. It made him sense for the first time the possible insignificance of terrestrial affairs. On some occasions he experienced in the evenings what he himself described as 'the coloured peace of sunsets'; on others, he felt disturbed by vague longings which he could not name. He grew conscious of his appearance and cared especially for his hair. The thought of going thin on top like his dad scared the wits out of him.

The girl he fancied was Gail Summers. Wherever he went he carried in his mind's eye the fling of her dark hair and the swaying of her body – these were things he could not forget, and to hear her laughing in the company of other people was like hearing laughter over the wall of a scented garden from which a time warp had excluded him. In his heart – figuratively speaking, of course – he conceded that if he had three feet she'd be his third shoe: but she was now going strong with some fellow from Bell's Hill.

Cinderella Girl
VIVIEN ALCOCK

Bella Jones didn't like Meg Hunter one little bit.
She was too rough, too noisy and too grubby.

'It's not only the way she crashes about, knocking
things over,' she said. 'It's everything about her.
She always looks such a fright. That great bush of
hair, I bet she never combs it. And her face is often
dirty. As for her clothes! She came to school
yesterday with those horrible green trousers of hers
done up with safety pins, did you notice? She just
doesn't care what she looks like. She's an utter
mess.'

It was true. Edward had to admit it. Yet there was
something he liked about Meg, a sort of warm glow,
a friendliness. She laughed a lot. The smaller kids
loved her.

Meg was young for her age, that was the trouble,
a big untidy girl with shaggy brown hair, like an
overgrown puppy. She still climbed the trees on the
common and rolled down the steep grass bank as
he had done when he was a kid. He even saw her
playing football with the boys from their old
primary school, and had been tempted for a
moment to join in. But the ground was wet and
muddy, and he was wearing his new trousers. Also
his mother was with him.

His mother liked people to look nice. 'It only
takes a little effort to look clean and tidy,' she was

fond of telling Edward, 'and it makes all the difference to what people think of you. Always remember that, Edward.' He knew she didn't approve of Meg. She never said so outright, but he could tell. Her plucked eyebrows always rose when she saw her, and she'd shake her head, as if to say, 'Well, really!'

'Isn't that Meg Hunter over there, playing football with those boys?' she'd asked. 'Covered in mud, poor girl. Just look at her! It's odd because her mother is really very nice, you know. And the two older girls are always beautifully dressed. You'd never take them for the same family. I wonder Mrs Hunter lets Meg go around looking like that.'

'She's Meg's stepmother,' Edward told her.

'It's not always easy being a stepmother,' his mother said. 'I imagine Meg can be quite a handful.'

A Cinderella girl, Edward thought. Poor Meg, nobody cares what she looks like. Perhaps her stepmother grudges every penny she has to spend on her, and won't buy her new clothes or even a hairbrush, so that she has to use safety pins when her zips break and comb her hair with her fingers.

'She's in your class, isn't she?' his mother asked.

'Yes.'

'Is she clever?'

'I don't know,' Edward said. 'I've never noticed.'

His mother laughed. 'I don't suppose you have,' she said. 'She's not the sort of girl boys look at.'

His mother didn't know everything, however. Edward did look at Meg, quite often. He wasn't certain why. She was plump and her clothes never seemed to fit her and she had big feet. On Sundays, however, when they met by chance in the park, they'd stay together, talking or watching their local team play football. He always looked forward to seeing her.

But it was Bella he really wanted to date. Pretty popular Bella whom a lot of boys claimed would let you kiss her in the cinema or in the bushes behind the cycle shed. He had never kissed a girl, not properly, and was beginning to feel left out. Of course they might be only boasting.

'Have you ever kissed a girl?' he asked his best friend Michael, who was tall and skinny and clever, and could be trusted not to betray him.

'Of course I have! Millions of times. Can't get away from them,' Michael told him. 'They swarm over me every Christmas. Mum's only got to put up a bit of mistletoe and I have to hide to avoid being trampled on.'

'No, seriously, have you?'

'My lips are sealed,' Michael said grandly. 'I'm not one to kiss and tell.'

'I'm not asking for names. Just a straight answer, yes or no.'

'No. What about you.'

'No,' Edward admitted, 'but don't tell anybody.'

Michael laughed. 'Don't sound so sad. We're still young. Far too young, my mum would say. Do you want to kiss just any girl, or one in particular?'

'I want to kiss Bella Jones.'

'Oh, her! I might've guessed. You always want to do what other people do,' Michael said. He was not one of Bella's admirers. 'Well, why don't you?'

He made it sound easy. Full of hope, Edward had asked Bella to come to see a film with him.

'No, I don't think so,' she said.

'Why not?' he asked. 'I thought you liked me.'

'Whatever gave you that idea?' she said.

'Oh, come on! There's a good film on at the Odeon. *Alligator Angel.* I'll treat you. What about tomorrow?'

She shook her head. 'Not tomorrow.'

'Wednesday?'

'Sorry. Can't manage Wednesday.'

'What about Thursday, then?'

'I dunno. I might. I'll think about it,' she said.

On Thursday morning, he came to school early, in his new trousers and his best shirt. But when Bella came, she told him she was going out with Kevin Clarke.

'But you promised –'

'I never promised. I just said I might,' she told him. 'Ask me again some time.'

So he asked her the next day, and the next day and the next, and every time she said, 'I dunno. I might. Ask me again.'

The last time she said this, he turned away without a word, and went to look out of the window, ignoring her. She didn't like that.

'What are you looking at?' she asked, coming to stand beside him.

'Nothing in particular.'

'Yes, you are. You're looking at Meg Hunter. Here she comes, late as usual. Doesn't she look stupid when she runs? Look at that smudge on her face! She can't have washed at all this morning.'

Edward knew how Meg got smudges on her face. Sometimes, when he was late, he saw her going along the road in front of him, trailing her fingers over the ledges of the buildings, stroking the dusty plastic dog outside the pet shop, then pushing her unruly hair back from her face with sooty hands.

'It's only dust,' he said.

'And what on earth does she think she's wearing? That cardigan's hideous! And it's coming unravelled at the sleeve. Why doesn't she make her stepmother buy her some decent clothes.'

'What she needs is a fairy godmother, a pumpkin and a prince,' Edward said.

'What she needs is a hot bath and a haircut,' Bella retorted, wrinkling her pretty little nose. 'Don't tell me you fancy her, Edward?'

Before he could answer, Mr Dunlock, their teacher, came into the room and ordered them to their places. Edward saw Meg, trying to slip unnoticed into the room, trip over someone's leg – whose? was it Bella's? – and stumble heavily against one of the tables.

'Late again, Meg?' Mr Dunlock said. He peered at her through his spectacles. 'What's that on your face? It looks like soot. Go and wash it off, there's a good girl.'

As Meg left the room, some of the girls giggled and whispered. Edward was too far away to see who they were. He wondered if Bella was one of them. She could be spiteful, he'd already found that out, but he didn't want to have to start again with another girl. He was used to being in love with her, used to asking her out, even used to being refused.

There was something to be said for unrequited love. It was safer. Often, in his sleep, when he tried to kiss Bella, he tripped over his own feet and missed her altogether. Once he dreamed he was sitting next to her in the dark cinema, holding her hand. But when he leaned over to kiss her, she suddenly turned into Mrs Trenter, their head teacher, who shouted angrily, 'Edward Walden, you've failed your tests! What will your mother say?'

Nevertheless it hurt his pride that Bella should keep on refusing him when she went out with several other boys who were not, he considered, better looking or more amusing or in any way nicer than he was.

'I don't mean to be conceited, but honestly!' he said to his friend Michael. 'She's been out with Kevin a lot, and he's the dregs. Why do you think it is?'

'The girl's daft,' Michael said kindly. 'She's got bad taste.'

The next Sunday, Edward walked moodily in the park, looking for Meg. He found her sitting in her favourite tree and climbed up beside her.

'Do you think there's something wrong with me?' he asked.

'In what way? Have you got a pain or spots or something?'

'No. I meant . . . Am I off-putting in any way? Have I got halitosis or do my feet stink?'

'No,' she said.

'If you were Bella, would you rather go out with me or Kevin Clarke?'

Meg laughed. 'Kevin Clarke writes her poems,' she said.

'Poems?' Edward repeated in astonishment. 'Whatever for?'

'She likes them. She sticks them in an album opposite photographs of herself, and shows them to us.'

'Good grief,' Edward said, appalled by this new slant on his beloved. 'What are they about?'

'They're all about her, of course,' Meg told him. 'You know the sort of thing:

'Oh, Bella's hair is brighter than the sun,

And Bella's eyes are bluer than the sky –'

'What rot!' Edward said in disgust. 'It's not even true. Bella's hair is pretty enough but I bet it's never ripened any tomatoes. I wonder she can stomach such tripe. She must be terribly vain.'

Meg didn't say anything.

'*You* wouldn't want anyone to write poems to you, would you, Meg?' he asked.

'I don't know. Just once, perhaps. But nobody ever will,' she said. He thought she sounded a bit wistful.

'I'll write you a poem, if you like,' he offered. 'Not that I'm any good at it, but I bet I can do as well as Kevin. Shall I?'

'Don't say that my hair will ripen tomatoes because it won't,' she said, pushing it back from her face and leaving a smudge on her nose. 'It might do to plant mustard and cress in. Mum's always trying to persuade me to have it cut.'

'I shall be strictly truthful,' he promised.

'Oh dear.'

After a moment, he began:

'Your hair is rough and long and needs a cut,
Your eyes are . . .'

'What colour are your eyes, Meg? I can't remember. Look at me, please.'

She turned her head. Her eyes were a greenish hazel and very bright. They reminded him of the sea at Cosheston, sparkling over the pebbles in the sunlight . . .

'Your mermaid eyes are flecked with gold and
    green.
Your nose is smudged, your sleeve unravelled
    but

Of all the girls at school you are my queen.'

He shouldn't have said that last line. It wasn't
true, was it? What about Bella? Besides, he couldn't
date Meg. His mother would have a fit and
everybody at school would tease him. He looked at
her anxiously, hoping she wouldn't take it
seriously, but she only laughed and told him it was
a splendid poem, far better than any of Kevin's.
  'Don't worry,' she said. 'I won't tell Bella.'

At the end of term, their school had a summer
disco in the assembly hall. Edward didn't think he'd
go. He had given up asking Bella to come out with
him, and no longer dreamed of her at night. So he
was surprised when she came up to him and said,
'Aren't you going to ask if you can take me to the
summer disco, Edward?'
  'You don't need anyone to go with. You can just
go,' he told her.
  'I know that,' she said. 'I just thought you might
want to call for me so we could go together.'
  He looked at her suspiciously. 'Would you come
with me if I asked you?'
  'I dunno. I might,' she said and ran off, giggling.
  'And I might ask some other girl,' he said, and
walked off. He knew whom he was going to ask. It
was only when he found Meg in the library that it
occurred to him that she might refuse.
  'Please,' he asked, as she hesitated.
  'I thought you'd ask Bella Jones,' she said.
  'No. I'm asking you.'
  'I can't dance,' she said. 'I've never been to a
disco.'
  'Nor have I,' he told her and they smiled at one
another.

He was nervous, standing outside the school on the Saturday of the party. Sometimes he was afraid Meg would not come after all, and Bella would laugh. Sometimes he was afraid Meg would come in her old green trousers, still done up with a safety pin, with her hair unbrushed and her face smudged, and Bella would laugh even louder. Bella had arrived with Kevin Clarke, and they were waiting in the entrance, looking at him and sniggering; Bella with her yellow hair frizzed out and her claws sharpened.

'Who are you waiting for, Edward?' she called out, but just then a big silver car drew up outside the school gates, and a girl in a sea-green dress got out. Her long brown hair was sleek and shining, earrings sparkled in her ears and there were silver buckles on her shoes. As she walked towards them, the thin material of her dress swirled out like the waves of the sea.

Everyone stared.

'Meg,' Edward said, coming forward. 'Meg, you look fabulous.'

'Don't I look posh? I hardly know myself,' she told him, laughing. 'Mum and my sisters took me in hand. They've been longing to do it for ages, but I wouldn't let them. Mum's bought me a whole lot of new clothes, Josie gave me these earrings and Netta these bracelets.'

She was no Cinderella, after all. She was Meg, whose family loved her, enough to let her play football in the park and climb trees when she wanted to, and to do her proud when the time came. She's beautiful, he thought, and felt for a moment an odd pang of loss. Had she gone for good, the laughing, untidy, romping girl who'd not wanted to grow up?

'Don't change too much,' he said. Then, as she looked up at him, he noticed a small smudge of eyeblack on her left cheek. Without thinking, he bent down and kissed her, forgetting that Bella and her friends were watching until he heard the catcalls. He didn't care what they thought, not now. It was as if the kiss had broken a spell and set him free. Nobody was going to tell him what to think any longer, nor choose his friends for him. This was the girl he had always liked. The others could suit themselves.

The Favourite
JACQUELINE WILSON

We knew where we were with Miss Fennimore, our old art teacher. She looked the part. Her wild grey hair was always escaping her bun and coiling down her neck in question marks. As she chatted about shading and perspective she was always trying to catch up the straggly bits with tortoiseshell combs. She went in for chunky jewellery – strings of amber, clanking bangles, agate rings. She was chunky too, but she didn't seem to remember this when she bought her clothes. Her T-shirts were always too tight and her tie-dyed trousers were taut over her spreading hips. She wore sandals too. She trod from girl to girl in those awful open-toed sandals, and whenever she spoke to me I'd look down at her ridged nails and see the little corn where the sandals rubbed and feel depressed.

Mandy and Trish and the others sent her up a bit but Miss Fennimore was so good-natured she just laughed when they teased her. I didn't join in. I'm not one of the noisy naughty ones. I don't generally get noticed much even though I tag around with Mandy and Trish. I'm middling at most things and mousy to look at. Some of the teachers have difficulty remembering my name even though I've been in their classes for years.

But it was different with Miss Fennimore. It's the one thing I'm good at. Art. I don't really like the sort of art we do at school. I like my own private art, when I shut myself in my bedroom for hours on end with huge sheets of cartridge paper and my big Christmas tin of Caran D'Ache pencils and I draw imaginary lands. I people them with all sorts of weird fantastic creatures. I pretend I'm one of them, and I'm not a bit middling or mousy. But even though school art is boring I can do it OK. Mandy and Trish generally tease me far more than they do the teachers, but they both go on and on about my so-called artistic ability. Miss Fennimore was very encouraging too. She'd always spend twice the time at my desk. She said I had a real talent and she was sure I'd get into art school when I was older. She lent me some art books and gave me a whole set of National Gallery postcards.

I was grateful but embarrassed too. I'd wanted to be singled out at school and yet it made me go hot and uncomfortable. I wanted Miss Fennimore to keep on making a fuss of me and yet my tummy went tight when she approached, and I blushed when she crowded up close to me to point something out.

'Did you see Megan blush?' Mandy hissed.

'She went scarlet. She hasn't half got a crush on old Fat-Bum Fennimore,' Trish tittered.

I didn't have a crush on Miss Fennimore. I didn't even like her very much, though she was so kind to me. So I had mixed feelings when she announced she was leaving at the end of the summer term. She invited me round to her flat that summer so I could see some of *her* artwork, but I made some excuse about having to help out in my mum's shop. I didn't help out much. I didn't see Mandy and Trish that much either. They went on holiday together and met these two boys and went around with them all the time. I spent most of the summer shut in my bedroom, drawing until my felt-tip pens went dry.

When school eventually started again I was curious to see who our new art teacher was. When we filed into the big hall for Assembly I looked at all the school staff standing on the stage, ready to spot the new faces. And then I saw him. We all saw him. We all stood, transfixed. We couldn't believe it, even after Miss Parish, the head, introduced him. Mr White, our new art teacher.

We've had quite a few male teachers before, even though ours is a girls' school. But they've always been exactly the sort of men you'd imagine: beards and Hush Puppy shoes or balding and twitchy with sweat-stains on their shirts. Mr White was young and blond and smiling. Smiling at all of us. Smiling at me. He was glancing along the rows of girls, and then he saw me and he smiled, specially for me.

That was the way it seemed, anyway. Though Mandy and Trish and the others seemed to think they'd been singled out too. Everyone was whispering all through Assembly and afterwards the whole school was buzzing. It was Mr White this, Mr White that. How old is he? Do you think he highlights his hair? His eyes! That smile!

Hundreds of girls, all saying the same things. Hundreds of girls, all desperate for their first art lesson of the term.

'If only I was good at art!' said Mandy.

'I know,' said Trish. 'I can't draw for toffee either.'

They both glared at me.

'You lucky swine,' said Mandy.

'You'll be teacher's pet again, Megan. It's not *fair*. Oh wow! What wouldn't I give to be Mr White's little pet,' said Trish.

'Don't be daft,' I said, but my heart was thudding inside my crisp school shirt.

We had a double art lesson that afternoon. The art room had already been transformed. Miss Fennimore's prim reproductions of Old Masters had all been pulled down. There were huge poster reproductions of Matisse, Picasso, Cezanne, Van Gogh, so that the walls crackled with colour. There were postcards too, tacked into themed displays — portraits, pop art, landscapes. Mandy and Trish paused, eyes popping, at the nude postcards — plump pink Renoir ladies, marble Michelangelo men, anxious angular Munch girls, Hockney boys bare but for their socks.

'Is this what we're going to be painting?' Mandy spluttered.

'Who's going to do the posing then?' said Trish. 'Oh boy, let's hope it's Mr White!'

They started giggling hysterically and Mr White shook his head at them.

'Hey, girls, cut the cackle, eh?' he said. 'I thought we'd all do a self-portrait today, right? I've got some little mirrors here. Help yourselves, prop your mirror up on your desk so you can remind yourself what you look like, and then get started. A quick pencil sketch and then start splodging on some paint. I want to see what you can do.'

There was a little routine groaning and a few more giggles but everyone soon settled. Mr White was very much in control, even though he was casual and relaxed. Poor Miss Fennimore used to spend fifteen minutes or more getting everybody sorted out and started, but in next to no time everyone was peering into their mirrors and painting. Everyone but me.

I so badly wanted to show Mr White that I could

paint, that I was the one who was good at art, that I was special. But I didn't look special. I screwed up my face and my mirror image grimaced back at me. Pale, panicky, pathetic. I tried to make a bold sketch but my hand shook and had no skill. I started rubbing out my crude beginnings.

'Hey, no erasers,' said Mr White.

'But –'

He shook his head. 'I want to see the way you do it first time round.'

So I was stuck. I had to carry on, even though it had all gone wrong. It was terrifying knowing there was no going back. I drew such light timid lines they were scarcely visible on the paper, and when I started painting my pale watery colours blurred and bled into each other.

Mr White started wandering around the room. His wasn't the measured sandalled tread of Miss Fennimore. He bounced erratically in his sneakers, darting here and there. He laughed at Mandy's over-optimistic representation of herself as a cartoon Monroe, blonde curls and pouting lips and big bosom. He chatted to Trish for ages, showing her how to shade, leaning over her to pencil on her paper. Her portrait gained depth and Trish herself was painted pink.

I kept waiting for it to be my turn, though I dreaded what he'd say. But each time I thought he was approaching me he changed direction with a little squeak of his sneakers and started talking to some other girl. The bell had gone and we were packing up when he eventually glanced in my direction. He looked at my wishy-washy portrait and then sighed.

'I thought I said no rubbing out?'

'I didn't.'

He raised his eyebrows, as if he didn't believe me. I looked at my portrait too. It did look as if I'd rubbed it all over until I was hardly there.

'She really didn't, Mr White,' said Mandy.

'She's ever so good at art, Megan, isn't she?' said Trish. 'She's much better than any of us. She always used to be Miss Fennimore's favourite.'

'Well, I don't have favourites,' said Mr White. 'Megan is a competent artist but she's got to learn to paint with conviction.'

I felt as if he'd stamped all over me in his jaunty sneakers. Mandy and Trish were consoling, but I could see by the brightness of their eyes that they were also secretly thrilled. Maybe they stood more chance with Mr White now. Because no matter what he said, all teachers had their favourites.

I decided I didn't care. Mr White was big-headed and arrogant and he didn't know half as much about real art as Miss Fennimore. Why should I want to be his favourite?

I tried hard to impress him every art lesson all the same. I threw away my rubber. I started to draw with a darker pencil. I mixed bright bold colours and spread them thickly on my paper. I breathed in hard and bit my lip as I worked; I so badly wanted to paint with conviction. But Mr White generally found fault. He saw through all the little tricksy things that had thrilled Miss Fennimore. He was dismissive of my light reflections and dark shadows.

'Don't fuss so with all the flibberty bits,' he said. 'Paint what's there first. Go for the centre. Be bold, Megan.'

I was Megan the middling, Megan the mouse. I didn't know how to be bold. Though at home, shut in my bedroom, I drew a new imaginary land, a glittering golden place where I was a giant princess, and I had a prince too, a gold prince just for me, a prince made bashful by my boldness, a prince who would stride seven leagues in his sneakers just to be by my side.

I wasn't alone in my fantasies. I think every girl in my class had fallen in love with Mr White. Stories about him circulated the cloakrooms every single day. Mr White had put his arm round one girl. Mr White had told another she was cute. Mr White's first name was Tim.

Tim. I whispered it in bed at night. And then I went to sleep and dreamt about him, and my dreams were as bold as brass. But in the art room I pretended not to care. I forced myself not to look up when he came near. I carried on painting, even though my hand shook. And it was no use anyway. I simply couldn't seem to please him. He praised nearly all the other girls but he kept on pick pick picking at me.

Each art lesson seemed over in a flash, and then there was another long weary week to get through. I still saw him round and about school but they were only glimpses. Some of the girls tried following him home. He'd been spotted in shops, in pubs, in clubs. Then Mandy came rushing into school one Monday to say she'd seen him in Sainsburys on Saturday with his family.

'Yeah, honest! It *was* him. He spoke to me, for God's sake. He said, "Hello, Mandy." Anyway. He's got this little toddler with cute blond hair – just like his daddy. He said hello too. But his wife didn't.'

'Come on, come *on*, Mandy, what's she like?'

'She looks a bit boring, actually. Youngish and her hair was a bit of a mess. She was fat too. Yeah, OK OK, I know *I'm* fat, but she's sort of lumbering.

Well, she might be pregnant, I suppose. But she still doesn't look anything special. Not special enough for *him*.'

I hated the idea of this wife, this child, maybe children – but they didn't stop my secret fantasies. Mr White was still special for me. Just occasionally he'd seem to catch my eye and smile as if he knew, as if I was special too, but then the next lesson in art he'd snub me and scoff at my paintings and I'd sink back into despair.

I didn't know what sort of mark he'd give me at the end of term. Miss Fennimore had always marked me so highly. I'd got over ninety per cent in my art exam last year, and my form teacher had added a little 'Well done!' at the bottom of my art report. The reports were already circulating round the teachers. After our English teacher had written hers she stopped me at the end of the lesson and asked me to take them over to the art room for Mr White.

Mandy and Trish had rushed on ahead for their lunch. I went over to the art room on my own. Mr White was on his own too, pinning up some surrealist pictures.

'Ah. Hi, Megan,' he said, and he smiled.

I swallowed.

'Here are our reports for you to fill in, Mr White,' I said.

I handed them over hurriedly, my damp hands making faint stains on the folder.

'Don't look so worried,' said Mr White. He reached out and patted me on the shoulder. The warmth of his hand through my school blouse seared my skin. 'I'm going to give you a very good report. I know I've been hard on you – but it's only because you've got such talent.'

I felt as if I would faint with pleasure at his words. I turned hastily so that he couldn't see and pretended to look at the new pictures.

There was one strange dark painting of four girls in a midnight street – one lying naked on blue satin sheets, and three fully clothed in black dresses, their hair tied back with big ribbons.

'Like yours,' said Mr White softly, pulling my ponytail. 'And they all look so pale, so tense. Like you, Megan.'

He was so close his breath tickled my neck. I didn't know what to do, what to say. The art room seemed to slant and then spin, the colours changing like a kaleidoscope. I don't know whether I swayed or stumbled, but Mr White was suddenly holding me. His face blurred as it came even nearer. I felt as if I were blurring too. This was my dream. But it wasn't a dream. It was real.

He did like me. I was special. I was his favourite. But this was different. It was what I wanted. But I didn't want *him* to want it. I didn't want him to want me because that stopped him being special. It made him shabby and speculative. He was my schoolteacher, a married man with a family. I was a schoolgirl.

So I forced myself to act like one, though I've never felt more grown up in my life.

'Of course I'm a bit tense, Mr White, because I'm really worried about my report,' I gabbled. 'I've got to prove to my mum that I've got a chance to go to art school. She just wants me to work in the shop with her, you see . . .'

I chatted on desperately, and maybe he did start to see. He blinked and took a step backwards and started talking too. Relaxed and casual as ever, but I'd seen a flicker of fear in his eyes. He was scared he'd misjudged things, scared I might tell.

But I didn't breathe a word. Nothing had really happened after all – although I knew I could turn it into an elaborate story for Mandy and Trish. It would make them take me seriously at last. But I didn't want to talk about it. I was already wishing it had never happened. Wishing there was some way of rubbing it all out.

Roz and the Smiling Knee
RACHEL ANDERSON

How Matt Got to be Alone with Roz

'D'you wanna come and see something?'

'What sort of something?'

'Something beautiful I just discovered. No one else knows about it. Nobody.'

She was suspicious, as well she might be. 'What sort of beautiful?'

'It's not a thing. It's a place. It's really ultra. You wouldn't believe it.'

She shrugged. 'I dunno.' She wanted to go back to her pals on the far side of the playground. I went on trying to tempt her.

'This place, they're probably going to bulldoze it over, build on it, destroy it, then you'll never get another chance to see it yourself.'

'Where is it then? Bet I know it already.'

'Can't tell you. It's a secret.' Girls like secrets, I knew that. They're always having secrets. 'If I told you, you might tell someone else. I'll have to show you.'

'How far is it? because the break bell's going to go in a minute.'

'Doesn't matter. It's only English next. We could bunk off.'

That was my clinching argument, not the

beautiful place I wanted to take her to, but the bunking off.

'Oh, all right,' she said.

She always was a rebel.

Her proper name was Rosamund. That's what teachers called her in registration. But she wasn't a rose sort of person. She liked to be called Roz. She thought it sounded hard. She wanted to be hard. She wore big boots and thick socks even though they weren't uniform.

I thought she was the most well-sorted person I had ever known.

She just despised me.

And yet, perhaps she didn't, because here she was following me along the alley behind the library, past the back of *Chicken Lickin'* where the pavement's all greasy with chip oil, over the car park, down a path, to that secluded place which I'd discovered.

It was a tiny triangle of paradise hidden between a warehouse and a used-car sales yard with the river flowing along its third side. In this secret garden, the bright grass grew tall, and the tired old trees were hazy with pink blossom.

'See, it's an old orchard!' I said with pride, as though I was God and had made it myself.

I pulled a piece of broken fence behind us. Now no one would know we were here.

'How d'you know?' she said.

'Because of the trees. They're all apple trees.'

Petals were drifting down from the branches like pink snow flakes, and where the flowers had begun to fall, there were miniature baby apples the size of acorns already beginning to swell.

I was waiting for her to say, 'Oooh Matt. Ooh it's so lovely!' and go all soft and swoony.

She said, 'What d'you wannna bring me here for?'

I said, 'I thought girls liked beautiful things.'

She snorted down her nose, like a cross horse. 'Then you don't know much about girls, and specially not this one!' She kicked the lace-topped cow parsley with her DM's, then went and stood scowling at the river.

I couldn't have told her the real reason, even if I'd known exactly what it was and been able to express it properly. It was something to do with wanting to be alone with her, maybe to touch her, or to talk to her, and to see if she was as tough as she claimed to be.

From the day that I'd found the abandoned orchard, I'd had this vision of us two sitting under a tree with our fingers entwined, with the tall green grass hiding us, separating us from the real world.

I said, 'Would you like to sit down?'

'Sit? Down there? In all that wet grass? Not likely, matey. It's oozing with slugs and centipedes and stuff.'

I saw no slugs. I saw only the happy honey-bees buzzing from flower to flower just like they do on *First Stages in Science* on telly.

'It's just an overgrown mess,' she said. 'You know what, you're really weird.'

I knew she was going to despise me even more.

'Good,' I said. 'I want to be weird.'

I was ready to go back to school before they'd noticed we were missing when she suddenly turned round from glaring at the river and said, 'I know!'

'Know what?'

'A really brillo place, better than this dump, where we can have a really good time and pick up food and stuff.'

How Roz Showed Matt Rich Pickings at the Ferryman's Arms

Roz's notion of a good place and a good time was different from mine. A little further along the river there was a pub called *The Ferryman's Arms*.

'Kids can't go in pubs,' I said.

'Not inside, you bozo. Outside.'

There was a paved beer garden with tables and benches and fancy umbrellas where people could watch the river flowing by and pretend they were in the countryside.

But the people were careless. They all left something behind – half a bag of salt and vinegar crisps, an unopened packet of bacon scratchings, a handful of dry roasted peanuts, a full glass of tomato juice. On the ground there were other things – a ten-pence piece, a fifty pence, three twos, and an old biro. It was amazing the number of people who didn't finish up all their beer.

'Good stuff all going to waste,' said Roz.

As each group of customers went on their way, we moved in and tidied up the table.

Roz reckoned that the pub owners wouldn't mind.

'They ought to be pleased. We're being helpful, tidying the place up.'

But some scummy customer went and complained about us because all of a sudden there was a yell of abuse from the doorway of the pub and the publican began making it clear he wasn't interested in welcoming happy helpers into his beer garden.

'Come on. Quick, Matt. Time to get lost.'

How Roz Had the Accident

We began scurrying back to the security of the river. But Roz tripped on the edge of the pub steps, fell over with a thump, then slithered down the bank.

It was those stupid boots she wears.

'Ow,' she said.

'Get up,' I said. 'Come *on*. Everybody's going to stare at us.'

'Can't,' she said. 'I'm hurt.'

'Well, you can't sit there for ever.'

She looked as though she was going to cry. What an amazing fuss some people like to make.

Roz the rebel.

'You ought to see what rugby players have to put up with.'

She clearly wasn't intending to move.

'All right, stop yelping,' I said. 'Let me take a look. And I'll kiss it better for you.'

Carefully, like opening the stage curtains for the school show, she lifted the edge of her grey school skirt to reveal her knee.

We both caught sight of what there was to see at the same moment.

Just below the bony bit of the kneecap, her leg was gaping open, like a great ruby-rich cavern.

Her face went a yoghurty colour. She looked away. I looked some more.

I could see right inside Roz, like no one else had seen inside her. I had wanted to get close to her, to see her as she really was but, for goodness sake, not this close!

'It's a bit like a sort of smile shape, isn't it?' I said to cover my embarrassment.

It wasn't bleeding too much, less than a

nosebleed. Out of the smile came tumbling some bits of yellow stuff, the bright colour of sweetcorn. Little blobs of it, like you see on slabs of meat in the butcher's window. It was fat, Roz's fat. I wanted to stuff it all back in.

She was falling apart.

No way would I kiss her better now.

'It's not so bad,' I said, pulling her skirt back over it. 'Probably needs cleaning up though. Don't worry.'

'Don't go. Please. You won't leave me here, will you?'

Where was that hardnut rebel, now?

'Gonna get some help, stupid,' I said.

I knew the drill. I hadn't been in the Cub Scouts for nothing. If in doubt, run like hell without looking back or you're dead for ever.

I ran like hell, till there was a good three-streets' distance between me and that foolish lump who couldn't even run without gashing herself.

How Matt Had a Pang of Conscience

The dinner break was over. I sidled into the playground just as the second bell was going. It was easy. I could mingle in the milling mass and no one would ever guess I'd been out. I certainly didn't want anyone knowing I'd been anywhere with Roz. I was right off her now. In fact, she was already part of the past.

I'd been ready to come straight back once I'd shown her the orchard. So it was entirely her own fault that it had gone wrong. She was just a great clumsy idiot.

I put the whole sorry incident right out of my

mind, packed it away in the back of my brain.

The trouble was, I couldn't help thinking about her.

I knew she wouldn't bleed to death. She was too healthy. And she still had her voice. So, after a while, when I didn't come back, she could start shouting and someone would come and find her.

Probably.

And what if they didn't?

And supposing it had been *me* sitting there waiting for someone I knew to turn up?

Suddenly, I did something stupidly brave. After all, Roz was only human.

I did a U-turn in the playground and ran like hell.

She was still there, but not quite the same place. She'd got herself up off the mud and was sitting with her leg stretched out in front of her. She was prodding at it with a dirty tissue like a small child poking a dissected earthworm to see if it could be made to move.

It was gaping wider, no longer a smile, more of a red rictus grin.

'Sorry about the delay,' I said, businesslike, as though I was strongly in control. 'Phones all vandalised. Tried three.'

She said, 'Oh thank you, Matt, thank you.'

'Don't thank me,' I snapped. 'I haven't *done* anything yet.'

'Thank you for coming back. I thought you weren't going to.'

'We're in this together.' That sounded rather good so I said it again. 'We're in this together, and as I got you into it, I'll have to get you out.'

I didn't want to touch her but I gave her a pat on the shoulder.

'It's quite bad, isn't it?' she said.

'It's disgusting.'

'Will it need stitches? I'm sure it will. I can't bear injections.'

'I'll go and ask in the pub.' That was the second brave thing of me to decide to do.

The publican was a surly brute. He didn't want to let me use his phone.

'It's an emergency,' I said. 'There's a wounded victim out there.'

'Damned drunks.'

'No, it's my friend,' I said.

'You school kids!' He spat on the floor. 'I told you not to mess round here.'

Instead of letting me call an ambulance, he phoned for a minicab and paid for it himself. But it wasn't kindness. He just wanted to be rid of us as fast as possible.

'Take them to Casualty,' he said to the driver.

I didn't really want to go in the cab with Roz but the publican made me.

How Matt Got to Hold Her Hand

There was a macho mega-death she-doctor on duty, a tiny woman but with the attitude to pain and suffering of a butcher.

'Come now, dear. There's nothing to it. I've had masses of these things.'

Masses? What was she? Some kind of a masochist injecting herself for fun?

I saw through the green cubicle curtain how they laid Roz out on a white paper sheet on a high narrow bed. A nurse took off her boots and held her leg still. When they began preparing the needle

with all that conjuring-trick business they like to do
– filling the syringe, tapping it with a finger,
holding it up to the light – Roz nearly freaked out.
They might at least have done it where she couldn't
see.

Roz began to squirm around. I knew she was
trying to escape.

'All right then, dear. You win. Your little friend
can come in too, if you promise to keep still.'

Little friend, huh!

So I came through the curtain and stood by Roz's
head. Under the bright lights, I saw the little hole in
her nostril where she'd tried to put in a nose-ring
last term. No wonder there's a rule against it. How
could I ever have wanted to get close to this person?

Roz didn't cry. She wasn't that weak, though
when the injections began to go in – seven in all
because I counted them – I saw her eyeballs
swivelling in her skull. If they were supposed to be
pain-killers, how come it was hurting her so much?

'That's it, old girl,' said Mrs-doctor-mega-death.
'Brave smile.'

'Can you talk to me, Matt?' Roz whispered.

She waved her hand about. I think she wanted
me to hold it. That hand that I had so much wanted
to touch, only now it was limp and huge and damp
like a great wet fish from the bottom of the river.

I took it. So that was the third brave thing I'd
done in one day. I squeezed it and it squeezed back
a tiny bit.

The doc and the nurse went on clattering around
Roz's knee with their sharp steel.

'Please talk,' said Roz.

So I opened my mouth and let all this rubbish
come tumbling out, about holidays with my mum,
about our dog and the way it always goes to the

next-door garden to do its business.

I ran out of things to say.

'Go on. More.'

I was like some daft radio chat show. To make a change, I asked her about her holidays, but she didn't seem up to giving answers. She just wanted to hear me yattering on. I could have said anything I wanted. I could've said, 'I really like you, Roz.' But I didn't. Not any more. The mood had long since passed.

How It All Turned Out

When the mums started turning up, there was a lot of yelling and nagging and telling off to be got through. Eventually, Roz hobbled out, all bandaged up, to her mum's car. I think she was in shock. She didn't even say goodbye.

I didn't see her again for three weeks.

I really missed her.

The Scream

ELIZABETH LAIRD

The playground at the end of the park is the usual sort of thing. A couple of swings, a slide, a ramp for roller skating, and an old climbing-frame with metal bars and tubes, quite good, actually, if you're young enough for it.

I hadn't been down there for ages, and it was only by chance that I went past it that day. I was on the way back from my friend's house, and I'd decided to do a detour round by the High Street and take a look at the new video releases.

It was a dull, cold day, and no one much was around. The playground was empty except for a bunch of kids, standing in a group in the far corner, away from the swings and slides, almost out of sight behind a tree.

I nearly walked right past them. It wasn't what they were saying that stopped me in my tracks. It was the way they sounded. Their voices were tense with excitement. Filled with violence.

Four boys, about nine or ten years old, were standing round a little kid, smaller than most of them, taunting him and jeering at him.

'Little scruff, aren't you, Paul?'

'Yeah, didn't you know, his mum gets all his clothes at the Oxfam shop.'

'No, she doesn't. She gets the stuff Oxfam won't take.'

The kid called Paul didn't look like much. His face was grey and strained. His eyes were darting about, looking for a way out of the tight ring that swayed round him. He must have thought a gap was opening up, because he made a jump towards it, but too slowly and hesitantly, as if he knew they'd stop him.

They did. One of them lunged forward and caught hold of his collar, pulling it away from the kid's scrawny little neck with one finger and thumb, and pretending to inspect it.

'Wah, look at this. Disgusting! He stinks! His mum never does any washing!'

'Nah, didn't you know, his mum likes him dirty. She's dirty herself. She washes his head down the toilet.'

'You ever been to his house?'

'Who, me? Course not. Might catch something.'

'They got things crawling out of their fridge.'

'They got green stuff growing on their walls.'

The kid's face was puckering up.

Don't cry! I thought. Whatever you do, don't cry! Laugh. Say something cool. Walk away.

But he didn't. I never had.

'Get off me!' he wailed. 'It's not true! My house is much cleaner than yours. My clothes all come from Marks and Spencers. Look at the label if you don't believe me!' He was choking on his tears.

They moved in closer.

'Marks and Spencers! Yeah, sure.'

'It's true! Get off me! Leave me *alone*!'

They were pretending to stand loose and casual, but they were really as taut as guitar strings. They'd smelled blood.

'Leave you alone? We haven't touched you!'

'You starting something?'

'You want a fight, or what?'

None of them had seen me. I stood there helplessly, willing my thoughts across the tarmac, trying to get them into the kid's terrified brain.

Don't look so scared! I was silently shouting at him. Put your hands in your pockets. Shrug your shoulders. Smile. For heaven's sake, *smile!*

One of them flicked at the kid's shoulder as if he was brushing something off it, but the flick was as hard as a punch. The kid staggered backwards, and trod on the foot of a tall boy in a green jacket, who had been closing in behind him. The tall boy began to hop about, faking agony, clutching at his foot.

'He stamped on my foot! Go on, Des, get him!'

My own heart was pounding now. My hands were clammy. I knew what was going to happen next.

I could go over and stop them, I told myself. They're only small. I could take them on easily.

They had the smell of violence on them. I knew it. I feared and hated it. I didn't want to walk on, but my feet carried me away of their own accord.

The kid must have made some kind of desperate move, trying to pull away, or push through the circle or something, because I heard one of them shout, 'That's *it*, he pushed me! I'll *do* you for that!' and the others cheered him on.

'Yeah, go on, Des. Kill him!'

'Kick his head in!'

I was shaking.

He's got to learn, I remember thinking to myself. He's got to stand on his own two feet. But I knew the real reason that stopped me going in. I was scared of being marked out by them, scared of their dads and their big brothers, scared of them.

I tried not to hear the scuffling, scrabbling sound

of their feet on the concrete, but I couldn't help hearing the kid scream. It wasn't the kind of scream that kids do deliberately, to attract attention and get an adult to rush on to the scene. It was a scream of pure loneliness and terror. It was the scream I'd felt time and again, deep inside, the kind of scream that only dares to come out when all hope has gone.

I was already round the corner by the time I heard it, out on the main road. I stood still for a moment, not knowing what to do, feeling miserable, rotten and guilty.

The pavement was crowded. Women pushed past me, bumping their shopping bags into me. People were picking over the racks outside the shoe shop, and gawping through the windows of the TV shop at twenty identical football games.

It's too late, anyway, I told myself. They'll have finished with him by now.

A bus pulled up at the stop just beside me. I don't know why I glanced along the upstairs windows. Habit, I suppose. I always used to have to check out the number 93 before I dared get on, in case Steve was on it. And it just so happened that he was. I stood, rooted to the pavement, and watched him.

When I was seeing him every day, before he was expelled from school, he'd always had at least one hanger-on with him, some little crawler who'd do whatever Steve said, and laugh whenever Steve tried to be funny, but he was on his own for once.

Perhaps I'd grown, or perhaps I'd always thought he was bigger than he really was. Anyway, he looked smaller now. He didn't see me at once. He was sitting hunched up, his face white and pinched.

I'd never noticed before that he was really quite thin. His shoulders were narrow and his arms looked puny. I flexed mine. I'd been working out a lot recently, and swimming twice a week. I felt good and strong.

Then he turned his head and looked right down at me. For a split second he actually looked pleased, as if he'd been lonely or something and was quite glad to see a face he knew. He almost smiled. At least, I think he did. I'd never seen him smile before, so I wasn't sure what it would look like.

He snapped out of it almost at once. He lunged his bullet head towards the window, baring his teeth and staring hard at me through narrowed eyes, his fingers jabbing the air obscenely. He looked like one of those vicious dogs that bark hysterically and strain to get at you when you walk past the place they think they're guarding.

Before, whenever I'd seen Steve, I'd pretended not to notice him. I'd always crossed the road, or turned to look in at a shop window, avoiding him as much as possible, getting out of his way as fast as I could. But quite suddenly, for the first time in my life, I wasn't afraid of him any more.

You're pathetic, I thought. Stupid. Alone. Out of the action. Out of my nightmares. No more screams for me.

I waved at him. His daft face dropped, and he gaped at me. Then, before he had time to get hold of himself, I turned round and began to dart back, down the side street, away from the main road, towards the playground.

I was strong. I was ready.

It seemed as if I'd been gone for hours, but actually it can't have been more than a minute or two.

They'd got the kid down on the ground, and he was feebly lashing out at them with his feet. He had his arms over his head and was trying to protect himself from the stabbing kicks of the smallest boy, whose body was so taut with anger I could almost feel it crackle, like electricity, from the other side of the playground.

'Beat him up, Des!' the other boys were shouting. 'Kick him hard!'

It was Des I would have to deal with.

They didn't hear me coming. I sprinted across the playground, grabbed Des by one shoulder and spun him round.

'Stop that. Stop it, you little . . .'

The other boys, concentrating on the kid on the ground, looked up, startled. One of them had been spitting on Paul's head. He wiped a slick of spittle off his chin. They began to back away, trying to resume their usual casual, swaggering posture. I only saw them out of the corner of my eye. I was watching Des.

He was sizing me up, turning an insolent shoulder towards me, balling his fists.

'Get off! Leave me alone! What's it got to do with you?'

The others saw him squaring up to me, took courage and came in nearer again. If Des went for me, they all would. If Des backed off, they'd all be too scared to touch me. It was only mental force that would drive them off, not violence. They wanted violence. They were good at it.

I looked Des up and down, pretending to recognise him.

'I know you. You beat up small kids all the time.'

He moved back a step.

'Nah. You don't know me. Never seen me.'

'Paul pushed him,' said one of the others.

'He stamped on my foot,' said the boy in the

green jacket. 'Asking for it.'

'Oh yeah?' I looked down at Paul. He wasn't even trying to get up off the ground. He'd covered his head with his jacket and his whole body was shaking with sobs. A cut on his hand was bleeding. 'Him? Asking for it? All of you against him?'

Two of them dropped their eyes and started kicking the toes of their trainers into the tarmac.

'Four against one? Think you're hard?'

'What's it to you? Who are you, anyway? What have I done?'

A whining note had crept into Des's voice. I didn't relax, but I felt more confident.

'I've been watching you,' I said, and I found myself using Steve's old trick, staring close down into Des's eyes, moving my head gradually closer to his and forcing him to step back.

'My brother's going to get you,' he said, trying to bring the snarl back into his voice. 'He'll knife you.'

'Nobody's going to knife me.' I found to my surprise that I was enjoying myself. I bent down, pulled the jacket off Paul's head and dragged him to his feet. 'You're going to leave this kid alone, see? I'm going to make sure of that. You're going to be watched. You beat up anyone else and you'll be in trouble. Real trouble. Not just from me. You haven't seen my mates when they get angry. It's not a very nice thing to see.'

They were moving away step by step, cursing and threatening, their voices getting bolder and louder as the distance between us grew.

'I know you, Des,' I called after them. 'I know all of you. I've had a good look at you. Me and my friends'll be watching you.'

They didn't like that. They didn't like hearing me say Des's name. They speeded up. I heard their swearing get fainter as they went round the corner, and fade altogether into the roar of traffic on the High Street.

I turned back to Paul. He'd stopped crying. He was rubbing at his smeary nose with his sleeve.

'They done you before?'

He shook his head, not wanting to speak to me. I remembered exactly how he was feeling. Humiliation. Hatred. Shame.

'They're nothing,' I said, trying to make him look up. 'They're pathetic. You're worth more than they are. You mustn't show them you're scared.'

'Leave me alone.' He was threatening to cry again. 'You don't know what it's like. You don't understand.'

I went over to one of the swings and sat down on it, letting it move me gently backwards and forwards.

'I do, as a matter of fact. It used to happen to me. Even in this playground once. A boy called Steve. Not any more, though. Never again.'

The clouds were beginning to lift. A group of mums and toddlers were coming into the playground. Paul turned away to hide his red eyes. The mums looked disapprovingly at me.

'It gets better,' I said, pushing the swing higher. 'Much better. You see through them in the end, see how stupid they are. You'll find that out one day. Anyway, they've done you over now, and they won't do it again. They'll leave you alone. If they don't they'll have me to . . .'

'Oi! Get down off that swing!'

I looked round. I'd been talking to myself. Paul had gone, and in his place was the park-keeper, red-faced. I braked with my feet.

'Can't you read? No kids over fourteen allowed

in this playground.'

'Where? I didn't see a notice.'

'Over there! By the gate!'

He was used to dealing with thugs like Steve and Des. He was working himself up, expecting trouble. I'd had enough for one day. I wasn't about to take him on.

I jumped off the swing and put my hands up.

'OK, OK!' I said. 'Don't shoot! I surrender!'

I walked past him, smiling at the row of frowning mums.

'And don't let me catch you in here again,' he shouted after me.

I went out of the playground and the gate swung shut behind me with a satisfying click. I felt extremely happy.

'Don't worry,' I said. 'I won't come back. Ever.'

Down to Earth
JOANNA CAREY

I was thinking about Elroy today. The day I met him, the lift was broken. I'd been to the shops and I was halfway up the stairs when I remembered my mum's cigarettes. I was counting, I'd counted two hundred and eighty-six steps so I knew I was over halfway. I always count, I learnt to count on them stairs. I don't know why I still do it, helps you keep going, I suppose.

Anyway, I had loads of shopping; tins of dog food, bread, potatoes, beer and lemonade. Heavy stuff and the laundry. My fingers had gone all sort of numb and waxy-looking like they were dead, so I put the carriers down and shook my hands around to get the feeling back. I wondered whether to go back for the cigarettes. I'd have to carry everything back down again – I couldn't leave it there on the landing.

Mum would have to go without her fags. I picked up the bags and counted on up to my landing. When I got there my fingers were dead again. I dumped the bags down and rattled the letterbox. Nobody answered so I fished out the key. It was hanging on a string inside.

'You must be mad,' says this voice behind me, 'leaving your key like that. Asking for trouble.' I turned round and saw this boy.

'What's it to you, anyway?' I said.

'We just moved in that flat opposite,' he goes. 'My mum's made me fix a chain and an extra bolt. Security, that's what. She gets really nervous when my dad's away. I told her, at least you don't have to worry about people climbing in through the window when you're on the thirteenth floor.'

'You should get a dog,' I told him. 'We've got two.'

'My mum's scared of dogs,' he goes, 'anyway, I thought you weren't meant to keep pets here?'

'I better go in,' I said. I unlocked the door. I could hear the dogs barking, their toenails all slithery on the floor as they ran to meet me.

I shut the door. He was nice, I thought. He was all right.

'Is that you, Kimberley?' said my mum. 'Yes,' I said. 'Why couldn't you open the door?'

She had her head in the kitchen sink. She was trying to dye her hair again. Nearly every week she did it. It cost a fortune. She was always sending me out to buy the stuff but it never worked properly. She never did it right. You're meant to mix these liquids up together or something and it gives off this foul smell. She was always yelling at me to read out the instructions but I couldn't read it properly either. Grandad could have read it but Mum said it was women's business and anyway Grandad would've said it was messing about with nature — same as what he said when I went and had all my hair cut off.

Anyway, there she was. She got her head out of the sink, dripping hair colouring on to the floor. It was called Natural Deep Burgundy and you have to use Ajax powder to get it off, but we didn't have any. She wiped the edges of her face with a tea towel. Then she took one of the plastic carriers I'd just unpacked and put it over her hair to stop the drips going on her housecoat. She fixed it with a clothes peg and went to turn on the telly.

I put the kettle on and opened a can of food for the dogs. Is it true that dogs eat whales?

I got Grandad's razor and put it on a tray with the soap and a basin of hot water. I made a cup of tea, got the towels out the laundry bag then, along with the newspaper I'd bought back from the shops, I carried it all through to the next room where Grandad was propped up, all crooked, in bed. I set him just right so he could drink his tea. Then – like every day – I undid his pyjamas, put the towels down his sides and washed him all over; his face, his neck, his chest, his armpits and all that. Then I shaved him. Took me a long time to learn to do the shaving, I can tell you, but I reckon I was quite good at it. It was difficult, you see, with him being so stiff and uncomfortable. Soon I had him lying back back on his pillow though, all nice with his hair combed, his pyjamas buttoned and his teeth in.

Then I gave him the paper and I settled down beside him so he could read to me a bit. That's how it was most days. Grandad had been ill a long time. He'd had two big operations so he'd spent a lot of time in hospital and the doctors said he'd be happier at home with a nurse coming in twice a week. My mum though, she reckoned they'd sent him home to die.

'They should have kept him up the hospital,' she'd go, 'where they've got people specially trained. I mean, he could pass away any time, and then where would we be, stuck up here? It's a full-time job, someone like that and they've no right just giving up on him. It's criminal, that's what. I don't know how I'm supposed to cope with him.'

She went on like this the whole time but really it was me that coped with him. My mum wasn't any good at it, probably her nerves or something. When he had a bad turn she just got in a right panic and the rest of the time she got dead ratty with him. Like if he had – you know, a bit of an accident and messed the bed, what would she do?

Only fly off the handle and scream at him.

'You dirty old man,' she'd go. 'Lying there all day like Lord Muck. Can't you control yourself?'

When I was changing his sheets I could see Grandad's eyes all wet. It's a terrible thing, seeing an old man cry and it made me want to cry too. I mean he couldn't help it, could he?

I was in my primary school when he was first took bad and it was then I started caring for him. He was that ill I often had to stop indoors with him and I fell behind at school, specially with reading. When I went to the comprehensive they had this special unit and it was quite good but I didn't go that often. Then they sent me to this other place and this teacher came to fetch me but my mum thought she was from the social services and give her a right blistering about Grandad. 'That's right,' she was yelling. 'You interfering busybodies, always telling me what's best for my Kimberley; well, it's her grandad you ought to be thinking of, he's the one that needs interfering with. Get him back up the hospital then maybe Kimberley'll stop bunking off school.'

I never said anything. I went up the centre sometimes when I had the time. It wasn't bad but I never could see the point. My job was at home, looking after Grandad. I knew I was good at that. Mum knew it too and so did Grandad.

We looked through the paper together. Grandad read some bits out then he settled to do the crossword while I went off to get his dinner. Then the letterbox rattled. I went to answer it. I had to grab the dogs, they were skidding past me in the passage. I opened the door. It was the boy from over the way.

'They've mended the lift,' he goes. 'I thought I'd let you know, in case – well, just in case you had any more shopping to do –' He stopped – he was sort of waving his hands around, a bit awkward, really.

'Oh, right,' I said. I was surprised. I mean, people don't usually come to the door just to be helpful, do they? The dogs were getting desperate and I had a job to hang on to them. I said to him, 'They haven't been out in ages. I haven't had a chance and my mum, she can't really handle them.'

'Tell you what,' he goes, 'why don't we take them for a walk?'

'You better come in then,' I said. 'I've got to get my grandad his dinner.'

'We went in the living room. My mum was there. I wished she didn't have that carrier bag on her head. She had the broom. She was sweeping the floor round the edges. The telly was on.

'Who's this, then?' she said.

'My name's Elroy,' said the boy.

'Oh yes,' goes my mum. 'What's the L stand for?'

Elroy didn't take no notice, he just said, 'We thought we might take the dogs out for a run.'

'Not before time,' said my mum and it was then I saw what it was she was sweeping up. And so did Elroy. It was dried-up dog mess. There was four or five of them behind the telly near the glass door that opens on to a sort of balcony. All the flats have got these balconies – there's a metal barrier round them with a little gap at the bottom. I lost my shoe through that gap when I was four. I watched Elroy watching my mum as she swept together a little pile of dog messes; they were nice and hard so they swept up quite easy. Then she dragged back the net curtain, opened the door and, with the broom, quick as a flash, whooshed them out the door and off the balcony.

I could imagine the noise as they hit the tops of the cars parked down there, but we was too high up to hear anything. It was awful.

Elroy looked at me, out the corner of his eye, then he said, 'You get a nice view from here, much better than round our side. Look – you can see St Paul's Cathedral. I went there once with my school. Prince William or somebody, he got married there.'

'I don't know about that,' said my mum. 'But I do know that I like my privacy,' and she slammed the door shut and pulled the nets back.

Quickly I got Grandad's sandwich ready and I took it to him with a glass of stout and his pills.

'Anything from the shops, Grandad?' I asked him.

'Yes, love, bring the motor magazine if they've got it, would you? Then we can look at it tonight.'

'And the cigarettes you forgot this morning,' said my mum, 'and you can pick up the washing from the launderette. Oh, and you'd better cash that giro.'

So I went off with Elroy. Just me, him and the dogs. It was really nice. And the lift was working. And it wasn't raining.

'What school do you go to?' I asked him in the lift.

'Well,' he said doing this funny sort of sideways look, 'I go to St Edwards, I got transferred there when we moved. Tell the truth though, I've been bunking off the last couple of days and that's when I saw you round the flats. Tell you what though, when I was coming up the stairs behind you, I thought you was a boy.'

Well, I didn't mind. Not really. And he made that funny face again, sort of smiling and looking to one side.

'She keeps you busy, your mum,' he said, as we went across the estate.

'Well,' I told him, 'somebody's got to look after Grandad. Mum doesn't really want him at home. She loves him and all that but she's not much good at that sort of thing; she's scared he's going to die at home. Grandad though, he hates it away from home, he's scared of dying in hospital. He likes me taking care of him – sensible, he calls me, down to earth – so I suppose it's up to me. Anyway, I like Grandad. I like being with him. He's a bit of a nuisance, I suppose, but really he's not half as bad as my mum, specially now she stops indoors with her nerves the whole time.'

I felt a bit stupid, doing all this talking. But it was nice. It was nice the way he listened to me.

'What's your mum like?' I asked him.

'Well,' goes Elroy, 'not much like yours. She's out a lot of the time, she works up west and when she's at home she's always cooking, cleaning, sewing, all that stuff. I think she makes herself busy just to show me and my dad how lazy we are.'

'How lazy?' I asked him.

'Well,' he said, 'just don't let her find out about me bunking off school, OK?'

We'd walked quite a long way. The dogs had disappeared. I did a brilliant whistle with my fingers and the dogs came running.

'How d'you do that?' said Elroy and we spent the next half-hour laughing and joking and whistling on each others' fingers. We followed the dogs round to the piles of rubbish at the back of the flats. I told Elroy about the other day when someone had chucked a kitchen sink out from the twelfth floor. 'You should have seen it where it landed,' I told him. 'It stuck in the ground like a crashed aeroplane.' And I told him about all the other weird things people chuck out here – last week there was a silver birdcage with a little dead budgie in it.

'You should get a job as a tour guide,' said Elroy. 'You could make anywhere seem interesting and unusual.'

I knew he was joking but I answered him seriously. 'No,' I said, 'I want to work in a garage, fixing cars and that.' It's true. My grandad, he was a motor mechanic, he teaches me all about it. He gets these magazines and we look at them. I can change a wheel myself. I changed the wheel on this man's car. He used to come and see my mum the whole time. Anyway, he had a puncture and he let me help him with it. It was really good.

The dogs had a proper run that day. Elroy whistled for them and after we'd fetched the washing and the shopping and that we went back up in the lift.

'We had a good time, me and Elroy,' I told Grandad while I was changing his sheets.

'I'm glad,' he said. 'I'm glad to see you having a bit of fun. I know it's not easy for you. And I'm sorry about all this –' he was pointing at the sheets on the floor – 'Don't tell your mum, will you? She gets so mad at me.'

'Don't worry,' I said, 'I'll take it over the

launderette tomorrow –' and maybe, I thought, maybe I'll meet up with Elroy again.

I did. Elroy'd had the same idea. He was there when I came out with the washing and we spent most of the afternoon together. He knocked for me next morning too, but I had to tell him; mornings I was busy looking after Grandad and doing jobs for Mum.

Afternoons were all right, though. I'd settle Grandad down for a sleep after his dinner and I'd see that Mum had loads of chocolates, videos, fags and stuff. Then I'd get the dogs and off we'd go. Elroy'd be waiting by the lift. We'd wander round the flats, play football or hang around looking at old cars. Once or twice we went to the river and let the dogs run on the mud at low tide. Elroy, he didn't talk all that much, but it was nice there with him, watching the birds swoop down over the water. I like birds.

'Sometimes,' I told Elroy, 'sometimes I see huge birds flying really high round our flat. But if you pull back the net curtains, they're often not birds after all – just torn bin-liners flapping about in the wind.'

Sometimes we'd get chips and eat them sitting on the swings in the playground, or we'd go round the back to see the new rubbish. One day we found an old bike someone had thrown out. The front fork was bent, the chain was broken, and it had no brakes. I told Grandad about it and he gave me some money and told me what to buy. 'You can fix it up, I'm sure,' he said and he lent me some tools from the box under his bed. Elroy and me soon had the bike going – it wasn't much good but it was OK for a laugh.

One afternoon we took it down the adventure

playground. Elroy, he went mad with it, racing it over the track and trying to do wheelies. The chain came off and got jammed in the back wheel. We tried to sort it out but it was no good.

'It was your fault,' I told Elroy, 'so you've flipping well got to mend it.'

'That's not fair,' he goes. 'You're supposed to be the mechanic – and anyway, it's your grandad that's got that massive great toolbox.'

We carried the bike back to the flats. It was heavy.

'Seeing as how it's unconscious,' said Elroy as we put it in the lift, 'we ought to have it on a stretcher.' Then he said, 'Tell you what, if we can't fix it, if it's a complete write off, we can do what everyone else round here does and chuck it off the balcony. It'll end up back where it started.' He was well pleased with this idea and he was laughing as he closed the lift doors. He put his arm round my shoulder and pressed the button marked thirteen. Nothing happened. He pressed it again.

'Guess what?' he goes. 'The lift's broken. Just our luck.'

It was quite a small lift and with me, Elroy, two dogs and a bicycle there wasn't a lot of room.

'Oh no – the door's jammed now,' he said. 'What are we going to do?' He'd put his arm round me again and he was jabbing away at the buttons but nothing happened; the door stayed shut. It was quite nice, all squashed up together like that. Then he goes, 'I was only kidding about the door – we're not really locked in.'

'I know,' I said and I punched him. 'What do you take me for – some kind of idiot?' Elroy laughed and he had this pen. On the roof of the lift he wrote, in green felt-tip, K4E and he drew a heart-shape round it. He was only kidding but I was well pleased, I liked that. It was really nice. We tried the lift again but it was no good. We picked up the bike and started up the stairs. The dogs, they ran on sniffing at all the puddles. They weren't tired but we had to stop for a rest on the eighth floor. Through a greasy window you could see right across London. The sun was going down.

'Look,' said Elroy. 'You can see that St Paul's. Tell you what, we could go there one day.'

'Oh, leave off,' I said. 'It's really late, my mum's going to kill me. Grandad'll be wanting his tea.'

I was knackered by the time we reached our landing.

'You better take the bike,' I said. 'See you then.'

I called the dogs and unlocked the door.

The minute I went in I knew something had happened. I could feel it. And the dogs, they felt it too. They put their tails down and they were whimpering.

I went to my grandad's room. He was dead. His head was right back on the pillow, his mouth open and the bottom lip all sunk in where his teeth should have been. His eyes were open. I'd made him some tea before I went out and he still had the cup in his hand. The tea was spilt across him. I leaned over to take the cup and it seemed almost like he was gripping it. I pulled the cup and a few drops of tea splashed my T-shirt like tears. Dirty tears, though.

I felt terrible. I felt so cold and lonely. He was gone but he was still there. Is it true that Jesus takes you away when you're dead? I didn't know what to do.

I found my mum. She was sitting in front of the telly. It was *Emmerdale* but the sound was off. She looked at me and she lit a cigarette even though there was one already going in a saucer on top of the telly.

'Well,' she said. 'So you've seen him. I told you so, didn't I? I said this would happen. Well, Kimberley, you've got a lot to answer for and no mistake. Where were you, I'd like to know. Where were you these last few weeks? Gallivanting off with that Leroy, neglecting your grandad, suiting yourself. Yes, my girl, you've got a lot to answer for. I knew it would end in trouble. I've had enough, you know, and what am I supposed to do now? He was my dad, you know, *he* was supposed to look after *me*.'

Then she said, 'And now the lift's not working. How can we get him down with the lift broken and him like that? He can't stay here.'

'Don't be daft, Mum,' I said. 'You know we couldn't take him in the lift, don't be silly.' Then, trying to keep calm and sensible, I said to her, 'Tell you what, Mum, I'll go round Elroy's and telephone the doctor. That's what you're supposed to do.'

Then she started screaming at me. 'Oh no, you don't, you're not going round that Elroy's no more, nothing but trouble he's brought us and, anyway, we don't want all his lot coming and poking their noses in here. No, my girl you can go over the surgery yourself and fetch the doctor, but not before you've seen to your grandad. Tidy him up a bit, we can't leave him looking like that. Come to that, if the doctor's coming I must do something about my hair.'

So I went to my grandad. He was still dead. I took away the tea-stained sheet. I got a clean one and I put it round him. I did wish I could have ironed it but really, once I'd straightened him up and tucked him in, he looked ever so peaceful. I combed his hair, same as always, and then cleared away the empty tea cup and folded the newspaper. I put Grandad's tooth glass behind the curtain, on the window ledge.

Then I took Grandad's toolbox from under the bed. It was heavy. I dragged it through into my room and pushed it under my bed.

It was then I heard this strange noise. It was my mum. She was crying. I never seen her cry, ever. She was sitting at the table shaking and heaving. Her hair was wet and I could see from the state of it she'd been putting more colour on it. Purply drops ran down her face as she sat there weeping. Her cigarette had gone purple – it was hissing. I mopped her a bit with a towel and I sat down with her. I wanted to help her, I wanted to talk to her. I thought we would be sad together but she was crying so much she didn't take any notice of me, except to sort of push me away when I tried to put my arm around her. So I went round Elroy's.

It was really nice in there, all neat with loads of nice furniture and stuff. Elroy was sitting at the table trying to fix the bike chain. His mum had put a newspaper out to protect the table top. I told him what had happened.

It was only then, telling Elroy about it that I, well, you know, heard what I was saying, and then I started crying. His mum was really kind, she gave me some tea. Elroy phoned the surgery. Then he came back with me to my place.

Mum was still sitting there. She was quivering. When she saw Elroy she started up screaming and crying again, telling him to clear off.

'I'd better go, Kim,' said Elroy. 'She's going to make herself ill if she goes on at me like that much longer. See you then, let me know what goes on.'

Mum went on crying. It was awful, she wouldn't let me near her so I went to sit with Grandad. He looked so grey and empty now I wondered if he had already gone to heaven. Can you do that, can you go straight away or do you have to wait until you're buried?

Anyway, then the doctor arrived. He calmed Mum down; he had to give her the needle, she was that bad. Then they took her away, they took her to a hospital. They took Grandad away too, and then my auntie came from Ruislip and she took me away. She said I'd be staying with her.

She explained to me that my mum had gone to a special hospital. She'd had a serious breakdown what with the stress of caring for Grandad all these years and looking after me single-handed, specially when I was bunking off school the whole time and staying out till all hours with some boy. It sounded like she was talking about someone else but I didn't say anything. There was no point. At least she told me I could bring the dogs 'for the time being' as she put it. So that's what happened. I went to my grandad's funeral, only they didn't bury him, they burnt him. Surely that can't be right. There was quite a few people, but I didn't see my mum there. My auntie came. She brought her kids but it turned out they couldn't handle the grief so my auntie sent them off down McDonald's till after.

Now I live in Ruislip. I'm sixteen now so I don't have to go to school any more. My auntie works full time so I help with the housework, do the shopping, and look after the kids. Lovely kids, quite a handful, though. My uncle, he's away just now. My auntie says they'll decide about the dogs when he gets back.

There's always loads of washing. It's when I go down the launderette that I think of Elroy. I never saw him again. I've still got Grandad's toolbox. I wonder if Elroy's still got the bike? Or maybe he chucked it off the balcony like he said.

What Does It Feel Like?
MICHAEL MORPURGO

Seven o'clock, and it was just an ordinary kind of autumn morning, much like any other. The mist covered the valley floor and the cows grazed along the river meadows. Sofia was still half-asleep. The wild roses smelt of apples. Sofia pulled a fat rosehip from the hedgerow and idly split it open with her thumbnail. It was packed with seed. A perfect spider's web laced with the mist linked the hedge to the gatepost. It trembled threateningly as she opened the gate into the meadow. She loved spiders' webs, but hated spiders.

Sofia sent the dog out to fetch in the cows and stayed leaning on the gate, her chin resting on her knuckles. Chewing nonchalantly, they meandered past her, ignoring her, all except Myrtle who glanced at her with baleful eyes and licked deep into her nose. 'Bad-tempered old cow,' Sofia muttered. And she followed Myrtle back along the lane towards the milking parlour. She could hear Mother singing inside, 'Raining in my heart', Buddy Holly again, always Buddy Holly.

Sofia wandered home, picking the last of the seeds out of the rosehip. She was deep in her thoughts. Mother did all the milking these days. She had done since Father went off with the other men to the war. He had been gone nearly three months now, and still there had been no news. No news was good news. Mother said that often. Sofia believed her, but she knew that was only because she needed to believe her. It was hope rather than belief. There was a photo of Father on top of the piano at home. A team photo, after the village won the local football league last year. He was the one with the droopy moustache and balding head, crouching down in the front and holding his arms out in triumph.

There had been little warning of his going. He'd just come out with it at breakfast one morning. Nan had tried to talk him out of it, but he was adamant. Mother and Nan held hands together and tried not to cry. 'There's five of us going from the village,' Father had said. 'We've got to, don't you see? Else the war will come here, and we none of us want that, do we?'

The fighting was somewhere down south a long way away, Sofia knew that much. People had talked of little else now for a year or more. She'd seen pictures of it on the television. There was the little girl without any legs, lying on a hospital bed. She'd never forgotten that. She never wanted to be without her legs, never. And at school, Mr Kovacs drew maps on the board, banged the desk, flashed his eyes and said that we had to fight for what was ours if we wanted to keep it. All of us had to fight if need be, he said. But until the day Father left, none of it seemed at all real to Sofia. Even now, she had seen no tanks or planes. She had heard no guns. She had asked Nan about the war – Mother didn't like to talk about it – about why Father was fighting.

'Because they want our land. They always have,' she'd said. 'And because we hate them. We always have. We've hated them for hundreds of years.'

'And do they hate us?' Sofia had asked.

'I suppose they must,' Nan had said.

Sofia remembered the last day Father had been with them. She had come home from school and he'd been there all smiling and smelling of the wood he'd been sawing. That evening was the last time they'd been milking together. She smiled as she recalled how Myrtle had whipped her mucky tail across Father's face. 'Bad-tempered old cow,' he'd said, wiping his face with the back of his hand. Sofia had laughed at the brown smudge left behind and Father had chased her out of the parlour. She thought then of his strong, calloused hands and loved them.

Nan was calling her from her thoughts. She hurried her through her breakfast, grumbling all the time that the telephone was not working, that the electricity was cut off too.

'I can't understand it,' she said. 'Maybe there's thunder about, but it doesn't feel like thunder.'

She sent her on her way to school with a whiskery kiss. It was ten to eight on Sofia's watch. Plenty of time. The farm was just on the edge of the village, not far. Sofia scuffled through the leaves, all the way down the road. By the time she reached the village square, there were no leaves left to scuffle. So she limped, one foot on the pavement, one in the road. She liked doing that. Sometimes, when no one was looking, she'd do the dance from *Singin' in the Rain*. This morning though, she couldn't. There were too many people around, but very little traffic on the move, she noticed, just a few bicycles. She crossed the road into the square. The café chairs were already out, and as usual Mighty Martha was scrubbing the pavement on her hands and knees. She looked up and blew the hair out of her face. Mighty Martha was the only famous person ever to be born in the village. She had won an Olympic silver medal for throwing the discus over twenty years before. Discus and medal hung proudly side by side on the café wall under a photo of Mighty Martha standing on a podium, smiling and waving. She was always smiling. That was why everyone wasn't just proud of her, they loved her too. It helped that she also happened to make the best apple cake in the entire world. That was why her café was always full, even at this early hour. She was smiling at Sofia now.

'Better hurry,' she called out. 'Kovacs will have your guts for garters if you're late.' Sofia turned into School Lane. She could hear the bell going now. She'd just make it. But then she stopped. It wasn't only the bell she was hearing. There was a distant rumble that sounded like thunder. So Nan had been right. There was thunder about. Sofia looked up at the mountains. It couldn't be thunder. There were no dark clouds. In fact there were no clouds at all, just jagged white peaks sharp against a clear blue sky. That was the moment Sofia remembered last night's geography homework: 'Mountain ranges of the world'. She'd left it behind. She fought back the panic rising inside her and tried to think. Both the choices open to her were bad ones. She could run home to fetch it and be late for school, very late; or she could tell Mr Kovacs that she'd left it at home by mistake, but then he wouldn't believe her. Either way Mr Kovacs would 'have her guts for garters'. Sofia chose what seemed to be the least painful option. She would fetch her homework, and on the way there and back, concoct some credible excuse for being late. She ran back across the square with Mighty Martha shouting after her, 'Where are you off to?' Sofia waved but did not reply.

The quickest way home was through the graveyard, but Sofia rarely took it. This morning she had to. She usually avoided the graveyard because Grandad had been buried there only two years before in the family grave and Nan went up there twice a week with fresh flowers. To pass the grave and see the flowers only made Sofia sad about Grandad all over again. There was a photograph of him on the grave that looked at her as she passed. She hated looking at it. She still half expected him to talk to her, which was silly and she knew it. Nonetheless she always hared past him before he had a chance to speak.

As she ran, her foot turned on a loose stone. She heard her ankle crack. It gave under her, and she fell heavily, grazing her knees and hands. She sat up to nurse her ankle, which was throbbing now with such a pain that she thought she might faint. When she finally looked up, Grandad was gazing at her sternly from his photograph. She tried to hold back her tears. He'd always hated her to cry. She rocked back and forth groaning, watching the blood from her knee trickle down her leg. Her books were scattered all over the path, her English book face-down in a puddle. She was reaching for it when she heard the thunder again, much closer this time. For just a moment she thought it might be guns, but then she dismissed that at once. The war was down south, miles away, everyone said so. Mr Kovacs' maps said so. By now she was hearing an incongruous rattling and squeaking, more like the noise of a dozen tractors trailing their ploughs on the road. She stood up on her one good foot and looked down into the village. Two tanks rumbled into the square from different ends of the village, engines roaring and smoking. Behind them came six open lorries. When they reached the square they all stopped. Soldiers jumped out. The engines died. The smoke lifted through the trees and a silence fell over the village. Doors opened, heads appeared at windows.

Mighty Martha stood alone in the square, her scrubbing brush in her hand. The soldiers were gazing around like tourists as the last of them climbed down out of the lorries. Mighty Martha's dog barked at them from the door of the café, his hackles raised. All the soldiers wore headbands, red headbands, except one who was wearing a beret and there was a gunbelt round his waist like a cowboy. The soldiers – Sofia thought there must be perhaps thirty in all gathered around him – then wandered off in small groups into the narrow streets as if they were going to explore. They had their rifles slung over their shoulders. Sofia wondered if Father wore a red band round his head like they did. The man in the black beret leaned back against a tank, crossed his legs and lit up a cigarette. Mighty Martha stood watching him for a few moments then she dropped her scrubbing brush into the bucket, slapped her hands dry and strode into the café. Sofia gathered up her books and hobbled down the path back towards the square. Mighty Martha would see to her ankle for her, like she had done once before when she'd come off her bike. She'd been a nurse once. She knew about these things; and besides, Sofia wanted to know what was going on. She wanted to get a closer look at the tanks. The homework and Mr Kovacs had been forgotten.

She had got as far as the toilets on the corner of the square when she saw Martha coming out of the café. She was holding a rifle in front of her. Suddenly she stopped, brought it to her shoulder and pointed it at the cowboy soldier.

'This is our village,' she cried, 'and you will never take it from us, never.' A shot rang out and the rifle fell from Martha's hands. Her head twisted unnaturally on her neck and nodded loose for a moment like a puppet's head. Then she fell face forward on to the cobbles and was still. The cowboy soldier was walking towards her, his pistol in his hand. He turned Martha over with the toe of his boot.

Sofia darted into the toilets, ran to the Ladies, closed the door behind her and bolted it. She sat down, squeezed her eyes tight shut and tried not to believe what she had just witnessed. She heard herself moaning and stopped breathing so that the moaning too would stop. But it did not. She knew then that it came from outside. She climbed up on to the toilet seat. The frosted window was a centimetre or two open. They were coming into the square from every corner of the square. Mr Kovacs and all the schoolchildren came in twos down School Lane, the soldiers hustling them along. The children seemed more bewildered than frightened, except little Ilic, who clutched Mr Kovacs' hand and cried openly. None of them had seen Martha yet. The cowboy soldier was climbing up on to a tank. He stood legs apart, thumbs hooked into his belt and watched as everyone was marshalled into the square.

The doctor was there, pushing old Mrs Marxova in her wheelchair. Swathed in a shawl, her face ashen, she was pointing down at Martha. Some people were still in their dressing-gowns and slippers. Stefan and Peter from the garage had their hands high in the air, a soldier behind them, jabbing them in their backs with his rifle barrel. Up the road from the bridge Sofia could see all the old folk from the retirement home, a couple of soldiers herding them along like cattle. They would pass by right underneath the toilet window. It was they who were moaning and wailing. Sofia drew back so she wouldn't be seen. She waited until they had gone and then peered out again.

The square was filling. The shoolchildren were gathered around Mr Kovacs who was talking to them, trying to reassure them, but the children had seen Martha. Everyone had seen Martha. Mrs Marxova held her hands over her eyes and was shaking her head. The doctor was leaning over Martha and feeling her neck, then he was listening to her chest. After a while he took his jacket off and covered her face. Little Ilic saw his mother and ran screaming across the square. One by one now the children ignored all Mr Kovacs' attempts to keep them together and went off to search for their mothers. Once found, they clung to them passionately as if they would never let go.

That was when Sofia saw Mother and Nan, arms linked, being marched into the square. All Sofia's neighbours were with them too. They'd even found Mr Dodovic who lived alone in his hut and kept his bees high up the mountainside. Like all the men, he too had his hands in the air. Mother went straight over to Mr Kovacs and took him by the arm. Mr Kovacs shook his head at her. Sofia longed to cry out, to run to her. But something inside her held her back. Everyone in the village was corralled in the square by now and surrounded by the soldiers.

A machine-gun was being set up on the steps of the post office and another by the garage on the corner. Mother was talking to the doctor and looking about her frantically. Nan had sat down in a chair outside the café and was staring blankly at Martha.

The cowboy soldier on the tank held up his hands. The hush was almost instantaneous. Even the children stopped crying except for Mrs Dungonic's new baby. Mrs Dungonic picked her up and shushed her over her shoulder. The whole square was silent now, expectant.

'You have seen now what happens if you resist,' the cowboy soldier began. 'No one will come to help you. All the telephone lines are cut. All the roads are blocked. You will do what we say. We do not want to harm any more of you, but if you make us, we will. Have no doubt about it. We are simply moving you. This land does not belong to you. You have been squatting here on our land for over three hundred years. You took it from my people. You stole it from us. Now we are taking back what is rightfully ours.' No one said a word. 'But we do not want to live in your stinking hovels so we are going to burn the whole place down. By this evening it will be as if it never existed. That way you'll have nothing to come back to, will you?' Still no one said anything.

Sofia was screaming inside herself, 'Don't just stand there. Tell him he can't do it. Stop him. What's the matter with you all?'

'Now,' the cowboy soldier went on as he swaggered along the side of his tank. 'Here's what you do. The men, if you can call yourselves men, you get in those lorries outside the shop. Be good boys now. Off you go.' No one moved. He took out his pistol and pointed it at the doctor. 'Go,' he said quietly.

'Where are we going?' the doctor asked.

'You'll see,' replied the cowboy soldier.

Sofia ducked down. A soldier was walking towards the toilets. Sofia prayed, her eyes tight shut, fists and jaws clenched. 'Don't let him come in. Don't let him come in. Be good, God. Don't let him come in.'

He came in. She heard the tap running into the basin. He was drinking. Then he spoke, 'Forgive me,' he whispered. 'Dear God, forgive me. I begged the captain. I begged him, but he wouldn't listen. Rats, he said, they breed like rats. You burn rats out. You destroy them. But they're not rats, they're flesh and blood. Oh God, oh God.' He was sobbing and then he was kicking the wall. That was the moment Sofia shifted her weight on to her bad ankle and slipped. The sobbing stopped at once. Sofia shrank back as the footsteps came towards her. She could hear his breathing through the door.

'Whoever you are,' his voice was gentle, confidential, 'whoever's in there, just listen to me. Whatever happens, stay where you are. Believe me, where they're going, you don't want to go. Stay put. Don't move. I'll do what I can.' And then he was gone.

It was some time after he'd left before Sofia screwed up enough courage to look out of her window again. When she did, she saw the last of the men from the village climbing up into the lorry. There were two lorry loads of them. A fierce anger welled up inside her. They were going like lambs, all of them. What of the rousing, triumphal songs they sung so often in the café? What of Mr Kovacs' defiant exortations that everyone must defend the homeland? How could they just leave the women and the children without even a word of protest? How could they? The men were just sitting there with bowed heads, Mr Kovacs weeping openly. She hated him then even more than the cowboy soldier. She hated them all.

'Good,' said the cowboy soldier smiling. 'Good boys. Now, women and children to the other lorries, and don't worry yourselves, you'll all meet up again soon enough. Hurry now.' He waved his pistol, and the women and children drifted slowly, reluctantly, across to the other side of the square. The soldiers stood by and looked on as they struggled to clamber in. Only one of them stepped forward to pick up the smaller children and hand them up. Sofia wondered if it was her soldier. She hoped it was. He had long hair to his shoulders and a moustache like Father's. He seemed very young to be a soldier.

It took three of them to lift Mrs Marxova out of her wheelchair and up into the lorry. They were not gentle with her. One of them kicked away her chair so that it rolled down the road, hitting a curb and turning over in the gutter. They laughed at that. Mother helped Nan up into the lorry beside her and they sat down together, Nan's head resting on her shoulder. The lorries started up. Mother was calling for her now, crying.

Sofia made up her mind in that instant. She had to be with them. Why should she trust the soldier? She didn't even know him. She hadn't even seen him. She unlocked the door and ran past the basins, forgetting her ankle. She slipped and fell by the doorway. By the time she was up on her feet again, she could hear the lorries already moving off. It was too late. Maybe, she thought, maybe the soldier was right after all. Maybe she was safer here, undiscovered. She hobbled back into the toilet and shut the door. She climbed up just in time to see the last lorry leaving the square and her mother's scarved head still turning, still looking, still crying.

The cowboy soldier leapt down off his tank. 'You know what to do. I don't want a building left standing. Understand? Nothing. You'll find all the petrol you need in the garage. Use hay, faggots, anything that'll burn. If it won't burn, then blow it up.' The soldiers cheered at that. Whooping and yelling, they scattered in all directions, some diving directly into the houses on the square and others running off down the village streets. Soon the square was left to the cowboy soldier who sat down on a bench and lit up another cigarette. He blew smoke rings into the air and poked his finger through them. Martha's dog was snuffling around her body, his tail between his legs.

Sofia could not look any more. She sat down. The blood had congealed on her leg. She took off her sock. Her ankle was puffed up and turning grey. A window shattered somewhere in the village, then another, then another. Some way away, a gun began to chatter and did not stop.

'Are you still in there?' came the soldier's voice softly from below her window.

'Yes,' she replied at once, without thinking.

'For God's sake, don't try to run. You'll be seen. They'll kill you if they see you. There mustn't be any witnesses, you see.'

'My mother, my nan. They were in the lorry. Where have you taken them? Where have they gone?'

'You don't want to know,' said the soldier. 'Just worry about yourself. And don't look out of the window. They'll see you. I could see the shape of your head from across the square. Keep down. I can't stay.' Sofia heard him walk away. She wanted to ask him so much more but could not risk calling out. She sat down on the toilet and tried to gather her thoughts, but nothing would come but tears. Racked with sobbing, Sofia put her head between her knees and hugged herself into a tight ball and closed her eyes. So she sat for hour after hour as they burnt the village around her. Trying not to listen, not to smell.

The first explosion was from far away, but all the same, it rocked the building, blasted her ears and left a ringing inside her head that would not stop. The next was closer, in the square itself, maybe the post office she thought, and the next shortly afterwards was even closer still. Perhaps the café. She bit her lip till it bled, determined not to scream, not to give herself away. When plaster crashed down from the ceiling on to her shoulders, she could stand it no longer. She lifted her head and screamed and screamed. Through her own screaming, through the whistle in her ears, she heard the whoosh and crackle of the flames outside, the roar of the roofs collapsing, and always the soldiers whooping.

Then she saw smoke drifting in under her door, smoke that would stifle the life out of her. She had to get away. She climbed up on to the seat and put her nose to the window to breathe in the last of the cleaner air. That was when the tanks began to fire from under the trees, pounding, pounding, pounding. She fell backwards on to the floor, back down into the smoke. She rolled into a corner, covering her face, her mouth, her ears, clenching herself into herself as tight as she would fit. Then she prayed. The picture she had seen on television of the child without any legs flashed into her head. 'Please God, I want my legs. I need my legs. Let me die if you want, but I want my legs. I want my legs.'

The smoke was thinning. Suddenly she could breathe without coughing, then there were voices outside.

'The toilets. Don't forget the toilets.' It was the cowboy soldier. 'A grenade will do it.'

'Hardly worth the trouble, Captain,' said the soldier, her soldier. 'It's not as if there's anyone left to piss in it, is there? And anyway, why don't we leave it there as a monument to them? All that's left of the bastards, their toilet.'

The cowboy soldier laughed. 'Good. Very good. I like it. Some bonfire, eh?' They were walking away now. The cowboy soldier went on, 'D'you see the mosque come down? Obstinate beggar, he was. Took twenty rounds to topple him. This heat gives a man a thirst, eh? Let's get at the beer.'

'Why not,' said Sofia's soldier.

There were no more shootings after that, no more explosions, but Sofia stayed where she was, curled up on the floor of the toilet. She could hear the soldiers carousing in the square and the sound of smashing beer bottles. One crashed against the window above her head, shattering the glass. Shortly after, their laughter was drowned by the tank engines starting up. They were calling each other. They were going. She waited a few minutes more until she was quite sure the tanks were on the move, their engines revving. Then she climbed up and looked out. The two tanks were rumbling away out of sight, belching black smoke out behind them. They were gone.

Everywhere she looked was utter destruction.

The village was a flaming, smoking ruin. Like all the other buildings, the café had no roof. Flames licked out of the windows, leaping across the road into the trees. The parked cars were blackened shells now, the tyres still burning furiously. The front of the shop had entirely caved in. Sofia got down, opened the door and hobbled out into the square. The minaret had fallen right across School Lane, obliterating the houses beneath. Martha still lay outside her café, but now her dog was beside her. He was not moving. Sofia sat down on the bench in the middle of the square where she was farthest from the heat of the fires. She had no tears left to cry.

She was still sitting there late that evening when the reporters came in their Land-rover. She was rocking back and forth and there was a cow beside her, grazing the grass. She was humming 'Raining in My Heart'. She looked up at them as they approached. 'Hello,' she said. 'That's Myrtle. She's come to find me. She wants milking.'

'Is this your village?' asked a reporter, pushing a microphone at her. Sofia looked at him blankly. 'What does it feel like to see it like this?' he went on. 'And what do you think of the people who've done it? Where the hell is everyone, anyway?'

'I've got my legs,' said Sofia, and she smiled. 'I've got my legs. God is great.'

The Simple Truth
IAN STRACHAN

'Lucy!' Mum called, as she climbed the stairs. 'Sam's here for you again.'

Lucy pulled a face at her own reflection in the dressing-table mirror. She was struggling with her unruly brown hair, trying to persuade it into a sophisticated-looking pleat. 'I can't be bothered with him now,' she spluttered through a mouthful of hairpins.

Mum stood behind her. 'It'd only take a moment. He's at the kitchen door.'

'But I'm already late meeting Alex,' Lucy said, viciously stabbing the pleat with a pin.

Lucy knew her mother didn't approve of Alex, but she believed this was simply because, at sixteen, he happened to be two years older than she was.

Although Alex was very dishy, with wavy black hair and glittering dark eyes, what really attracted Lucy to him was the way he smouldered with a casual air of danger. She need only be near him to feel electric currents tingling beneath her skin to her nerve endings.

Alex regarded girls as a tiresome, but necessary, accessory to his image and was well known for changing them as casually as Lucy discarded unfashionable clothes. But, although he undoubtedly gave more thought to trading in his bike for a newer model, girls continued to queue for the privilege of being chosen and eventually dumped.

However, despite his notorious reputation, Lucy was surprised to discover the nearest Alex came to any physical display of affection was when he draped a lifeless arm round her shoulders. Like leaving an arm lying along someone else's chair-back, it showed possession rather than passion.

Very occasionally, but only if the right people were looking, he would swoop down like a diving bird of prey and give her cheek a peck, but Lucy dreamed of the day when he would actually kiss her, properly, on the lips.

Her mother's secret dream was of the day when Alex would move away, preferably to another country! She saw Alex as a ticking time bomb and one she desperately hoped would not destroy Lucy when the inevitable explosion occurred! Strangely, she'd never suffered a second's worry whenever Lucy had been with Sam.

Physically in his twenties, complications which set in during Sam's birth had resulted in a lack of oxygen to the brain and meant he could never pass the mental age of ten.

From Lucy's birth they were inseparable. Sam helped Lucy take her first steps and by the time she was nine, and something of a tomboy, they were great mates. Sam's parents were rather old and he was delighted to have someone of his own age around. He taught her how to climb trees and build dens in nearby Betton Wood and, because he was exceptionally strong, Sam was especially good at lifting heavy branches.

True, some of the other kids thought Sam was a bit weird. Maybe because of his pale, constantly smiling face and thatch of blond hair, they called him Moonface, until Lucy chased them away.

However, during the recent summer, Lucy made an earthshattering discovery: she preferred being *with* boys, to behaving like one. The moment she started going around with Alex, Lucy, feeling she'd outgrown Sam, immediately tried to cool off their friendship.

But Sam insisted on still calling for Lucy, continually knocking on the kitchen door and asking, in his irritatingly innocent way, 'Is Lucy coming out to play?'

When that failed, he tried to tempt her out with presents: a sticky sweet coated with pocket fluff, a newt in a margarine container, or a wilted bunch of wild flowers he'd picked from the wood.

Although Lucy suffered minor twinges of guilt about Sam, she told herself, even if he would never grow up, she couldn't spend the rest of her life building dens!

Besides, Sam wasn't a real boy, unlike Alex. Sam was just . . . Sam.

But he refused to understand and, apart from school, wherever she went, Sam trotted after her like a clumsy, devoted dog.

Lucy nearly died of shame when he followed her into town one day! While she talked to Alex outside Tasti Snax, Sam stood silently watching her from the opposite side of the street, until Alex demanded, 'Who's that over there, Luce, staring at you?'

Without glancing at Sam, Lucy shrugged and lied, 'I've never seen him before.'

'D'you think he's a bit simple, or something?'

'I just said,' Lucy snapped, 'I don't know him!'

That was the first time Lucy hadn't stuck up for Sam, but when Sam next tried to follow her, Lucy yelled at him, 'Just stay away from me! Got it?'

Sam's smile had flickered uncertainly like a failing light bulb, before being completely extinguished. Without another word he trundled off home.

After that, although Lucy suspected Sam still spied on her, he must have kept a safe distance between them, because she'd never spotted him, but he kept coming to the house.

'You know how much Sam misses you,' Mum said quietly.

Lucy spat hairpins. 'Oh, Mum! I look worse now than when I started.'

'Let me try.'

'There's no time!' Lucy jumped up. 'If I'm not there soon, Alex'll be gone without me.' She snatched up a crushed-mulberry velvet cap and hastily stuffed her hair up under it. 'How's that?'

Mum looked uneasy. It wasn't the cap that bothered her, more the skin-tight, white leggings. She couldn't help wishing Lucy's black baggy sweater had been a little longer, but she forced a smile. 'You look smashing!'

Lucy bounced noisily down the stairs, calling over her shoulder, 'See you later!'

'Where are you going?'

Pretending she hadn't heard, Lucy slammed the front door. She hated 'where' or 'when' questions. She didn't want to plan everything, the way grown-ups did. She wanted to be a free spirit, able to do things on the spur of the moment and act on impulse, like Alex.

'That's what being a biker is all about,' Alex told her, soon after they started going out together. 'With your own wheels, you depend on no one. You go where you want, when you want.'

Not that Alex's wheels usually seemed to take him further than Betton Wood, where he roared up and down the steep tracks, competing with other bikers in what Alex called time trials.

Lucy, who was expected to hang around admiring the dangerous stunts he performed, thought 'time' was the least important part. The main object seemed to be to show off, until everyone was splattered with mud and eventually somebody fell off, his engine whining in protest.

Afterwards, once the bike had been cleaned off, usually by Lucy, and lovingly polished by Alex, he was mostly found leaning against it, posing in matching lime-green leathers and helmet for the benefit of the gaggle of girls who inhabited the steamed-up window of Tasti Snax.

Which was where Lucy had arranged to meet him. Though 'arranged' was perhaps too strong a word for Alex, who never liked being tied down.

'Will I see you at Tasti Snax tomorrow night?' Lucy asked each evening, as he dropped her off at the end of their road to avoid Lucy's mother finding out she'd illegally been riding pillion and without a safety helmet.

'Maybe,' was Alex's regular, off-hand reply. 'Catch you later!' With an airy wave of his gauntleted hand, Alex always accelerated violently, executed a wheelie and roared off down the road.

Lucy, nostrils filled with the acrid smell of burned rubber, was left staring at his black skid mark, while the neighbourhood dogs barked their protests.

When she arrived outside Tasti Snax the church clock was striking six, but there was no sign of his 'lean, green, mean machine' or of Alex.

If she'd worn trainers and jeans she could have

run, but the heels of her new, fashionable boots made that impossible. Besides, looking like Sally Gunnell after a record-breaking dash, wasn't part of her new image.

She pushed open the door and was hit by a wave of cigarette smoke combined with the fumes from over-heated chip fat.

'Coke, please,' Lucy said.

Without a word, Bernie, a short, dumpy man, whose clothes looked as if they'd been dunked in his own chip fat, poured the liquid and swept up the coins she left on the damp counter.

'Have you seen Alex?' Lucy asked.

'Uh? Oh, him! Yeah, he was in earlier.' Bernie's lip curled. 'Spent two hours drinking one coke!'

'Where's he gone?'

'I don't know and I don't care! Customers like him keep this place full up without me making a penny!' He roared through the hatch at his mouse-like wife, 'Must I die of old age, waiting for toast?'

Bernie was right about the crowd. There wasn't an empty seat. Seeing her problem, one boy called out, 'You can park a beautiful bum like yours on my knee, darlin'!'

Trying not to blush and ignoring his mates' lewd laughter, Lucy self-consciously walked towards the window. The outfit she'd chosen solely for Alex's benefit, suddenly left her feeling very exposed.

From the window table, a girl with frizzy, ginger hair, called out to Lucy, 'Looking for Alex?' The others giggled maliciously.

They reminded Lucy of the women during the French Revolution, who sat around the guillotine, knitting while heads rolled. Blessed with the ears and eyes of MI5, they collected scandal and gossip, and got their kicks from breaking bad news to others.

Lucy shrugged. 'Not specially.'

'Good thing. 'Cos he left about ten minutes ago with jail-bait Janice on his pillion!'

Janice was an over-developed twelve-year-old with, like Superman, a tendency to freely expose her underwear.

'So I'd reckon,' Ginger Frizz continued, 'they were heading for Betton Wood.'

As they cackled, Lucy felt a stab of jealousy twisting in her stomach but, determined not to give them the satisfaction of seeing how upset she was, Lucy tried to take advantage of three lads sauntering in, to slip out unnoticed.

She failed. Before the door shut behind her, the eagle-eyed watchers burst into 'The Teddy Bears' Picnic' and their warning words, about not going into the woods, pursued her out into the street.

She was still some way from Betton Wood when she caught the echoing whine of the bike engines. Though Lucy would have happily travelled to the ends of the earth to meet Alex, she wished he'd said he was going to be there in the first place, so that she needn't have wasted precious time pounding into town!

And why had he left with Janice, of all people? Was this typical of Alex – using Janice to tell her she'd been dumped?

By the time she reached the rough wooden stile which led to the main drive through the wood, the setting sun hung above the trees like a huge blood orange and the air was sickly with the smell of pine.

In the distance, screech owls squabbled while, far off, a dog fox barked, anticipating the velvet secrecy of the night.

Lucy wondered why Betton Wood never felt as friendly these days as it had when she used to go there with Sam.

Lucy climbed the stile and swore when a splinter snagged her leggings, drawing a thread out into an ugly hole.

Although finding Alex was mainly a matter of listening for the roar of the engines, the growing twilight amongst the trees made it increasingly difficult to see where she was walking on the uneven track. Lucy missed her footing, lost her balance, and stumbled into a pothole of muddy water. As she fell, the branch of a young conifer scratched her face and flicked the cap off her head.

'Oh, no!' Lucy wailed. Not only had her hair escaped, but there were mud spots up her legs. 'By the time I reach Alex I'll look like a bag lady.'

Suddenly, behind her, in the fringe of the wood, a twig snapped under the pressure of a foot.

'Who's there?' she demanded. In the gathering gloom, it was impossible to see anyone. Her voice quavered slightly as she called out, hopefully, 'Alex? Stop messing about, I know it's you.' But when she got no reply, Lucy panicked.

Blindly, she ran towards the sound of the bikes. Lucy forced her way through the branches and brambles which tugged at her, only too aware of the heavy footsteps following close behind.

When she burst out of the trees, Lucy was going so fast she almost ended up under Alex's front wheel.

He braked violently and the bike began to slip from under him, its back wheel sending up an arc of mud. 'Watch it, Luce!' he shouted, angrily.

She hated the way Alex always shortened her name and was secretly pleased by the way his mates jeered as Alex struggled to right the bike and pull up.

Switching off the engine, he whipped off his helmet and mud-splattered goggles to get a better look at Lucy, who was trapped in the beam of his headlight. 'Look at the state of you!'

Lucy's tangled hair fell about her face as she glanced down at her ruined outfit. Her boots were scuffed and caked with mud. The once-white leggings were not only mud-splattered but streaked with the powdery, green lichen, which had rubbed off the branches she'd pushed past.

Miserable and breathless, Lucy fought back her tears. 'Somebody was chasing me!'

'Leave it out, Luce!' Alex said scornfully. 'Us bikers are the only people up here.' But when Alex realised his mates, bored by a second's inactivity, were already racing off towards the town without him, he added with a grin, 'Seems there's only us two now.'

But after everything Lucy had gone through she wasn't letting Alex off that easily. 'So, where's Janice then?'

'Janice? What are you on about? I only gave her a lift home, didn't I?' Alex switched off the bike's headlight, kicked down its stand and walked over to Lucy. 'I don't need to settle for plain bread, when I can have jam on it!'

In spite of knowing she looked like something the cat had played with, Lucy felt quite flattered. 'I was really scared just now.'

'Give over! You've no need to be scared, Luce, not when I'm here.' Lucy felt the old familiar tingle of excitement beginning to return. 'Nothing's going to hurt you,' he said firmly.

Before she knew what was happening, his arms

suddenly snaked round under her sweater and he jerked Lucy heavily against him.

'Hey!'

'Time for talking's over,' he said abruptly and lunged forward into a kiss.

But this was nothing like the passionate but tender embrace Lucy had longed for. His lips and teeth bruised hers so painfully that, as he wormed his tongue into her mouth, the flavour of his favourite tortilla chips mingled with the taste of her own blood.

Lucy struggled out of his grip. 'Don't do that!' she said, taking several steps back.

'What's your problem?' Alex rasped. 'You know you've been dying for this!'

As Alex lunged towards her, Lucy screamed.

But Alex never arrived. From behind a bush, Sam leapt between them and Alex collided with him as violently as a train hitting buffers.

Alex shouted at Lucy, 'What's this maniac doing here?'

'Don't call him names!' Lucy shouted. 'Sam's my friend.'

'Funny friends you've got!' Alex muttered and then, trying to bluff his way out, he said to Sam, 'Clear off, back where you belong.'

But Sam, who was centimetres taller than Alex, folded his arms and shook his head, but he was still smiling at Alex as he said, 'I won't let you hurt Lucy.'

'Don't be daft,' Alex laughed, uneasily. 'We know what we're doing, don't we, Luce? Run along home, son.' Alex tried to ignore Sam by walking round him towards Lucy.

Believing Sam had given up the fight, Lucy was horrified when she saw, over Alex's shoulder, that he'd picked up a branch and, although he was still smiling, seemed about to smash it down on Alex's head. 'Sam, no!'

Alex swung round. 'Are you crazy?'

Sam shook his head. 'No, *I'm* not! But maybe you are, for staying where you're not wanted.'

'I'm not afraid of you, that's for sure!'

Lucy, who knew far better than Alex exactly how strong Sam was, was terrified Sam would do something violent. Although she knew Alex deserved it, she also realised Sam would be the one who got into trouble. 'Drop it, Sam!'

Sam looked at her carefully for a moment and then, with a cheerful grin, said, 'If you say so, Lucy.'

He swung the branch down so heavily, not on Alex, but on his bike, that it snapped in two, scratching the petrol tank's shiny green paintwork and leaving an ugly dent.

'You're barmy!' Alex cried, leaping forward.

But before he could reach his precious machine, Sam had found another hefty chunk of wood and was threatening to repeat the treatment.

'Stop that!' Alex shouted, rushing to protect his beloved bike. 'I'm getting out of here!' He tugged on his helmet and goggles and frantically tried to kick-start the machine, hoping to leave before Sam did any more damage.

'I would if I was you,' Sam smiled in agreement, still ominously waving the lump of wood.

But the engine refused to fire.

Alex, in no doubt that Sam was going to hit the machine again, slipped it out of gear and freewheeled down the hill until the engine finally caught and he roared off.

As the noise faded, Sam dropped the piece of

wood. 'I think we should go home.' When Lucy didn't reply, he peered into her face and found tears streaming down her cheeks. 'Don't cry, Lucy.' In trying to brush away her tears with his fingers he left muddy streaks. 'You mustn't cry.'

'But Alex was horrible to me, Sam,' she sobbed, 'and I thought he was so wonderful.'

Sam nodded solemnly. 'I wouldn't play with him again.'

Lucy laughed through her tears. 'Sam! You're fantastic.'

'So are you, Lucy.'

She took his big smiling face in her hands and, very gently, kissed Sam on the lips. 'Sam, thanks for looking after me.'

As they walked silently home, Lucy wondered how she could have been so wrong about Alex? She also knew it was time she really did grow up; Sam wouldn't always be around to rescue her from her own stupidity.

Sam was recovering from the surprise of being kissed properly by a girl for the very first time.

But, by the time they reached Lucy's gate, their silence had developed an air of sadness. The events of the evening, and particularly Lucy's grateful but impulsive kiss, meant nothing could ever be the same again between them. They would never be able to regain the innocence which, until that night, had been the cornerstone of their relationship.

By rescuing his friend, Sam had lost her for ever. Lucy had become just another grown-up.

The Mahdi Sisters
ADÈLE GERAS

'My big sister, my poor Leila,' said Yasmina, taking a dainty bite out of a small square of Turkish delight and licking her fingers, 'is in love. That's why she can't concentrate on doing your hair. Her hands are trembling too much. Not only is she in love, she is seeing her beloved tonight after a separation of two weeks. I don't know how I have endured it. You cannot imagine, Pat, the sighings and groanings that have gone on while he was in Dakar. But he is back at last, and tonight at the club dance, they will be reunited.'

I was sitting at the dressing-table and Leila was putting my hair up in a French pleat, ready for the evening. She made a face at me in the mirror, as if to say: 'Listen to my silly little sister!' Her mouth was full of pins for my hair, or she would have answered Yasmina at once. The Mahdi sisters had the kind of dressing-table I had only ever seen in films: covered in lacy flounces and with a mirror in three sections that allowed you to look at yourself from every possible angle. As for the make-up displayed on it, I had never seen such luscious pots of cream, such glittering cut-glass perfume bottles, so many lipsticks and eyeshadows, and mascara brushes outside Selfridges. I was entranced by Yasmina's powder puff (pink swansdown) and mesmerized by Leila's ropes of beads ('pearls, amber, crystal, and all false, naturally!') hanging over one corner of the mirror.

In England, I knew, I could never have been friendly with the Mahdi sisters, but this was what my father called 'the Colony': The Gambia, in West Africa, in the days before Independence, when the capital was still called Bathurst. Things were different here, different from what I was used to at home. I was fourteen years old and on a visit to my parents during the school summer holidays, and I was friends, *proper* friends, with Leila and Yasmina, who were grown up. Leila was twenty, and Yasmina was eighteen. My mother played bridge with their mother, and had taken me to their house almost as soon as I'd arrived in Bathurst. I'd been wearing a dress of cotton gingham, blindingly white ankle socks and my regulation school shoes.

'The Mahdis are Syrian,' my mother had explained as we stepped into a shady courtyard and, to this day, 'Syrian' conjures up a drowsy enchantment. Every cushion, curtain and tablecloth was made of velvet or satin, there were big brass trays, and tables of dark wood patterned with mosaics of mother-of-pearl. Mrs Mahdi smelled of attar of roses, and gave me wonderful cakes dripping with honey, and coffee out of a very tall brass coffee pot. No one had ever given me coffee before. Mrs Mahdi hadn't even asked. She'd simply assumed I would drink it. At school, we sometimes had milk flavoured with Camp coffee essence, but this was altogether different: fragrant, hot, sweet, and blissfully adult.

Leila and Yasmina came out to be introduced. I think my mouth must have fallen open in amazement. I had never seen such beauty in my life.

'Don't stare, Patricia,' my mother said. 'It's rude.'

'I'm sorry,' I blushed. 'Only you both look like princesses. You're very pretty.'

They wore lipstick and had dark lines drawn around their eyes. Their nails were red and shiny and pointed, and their clothes flowed silkily across their bodies. They had obviously never even seen an ankle sock. Their naked feet (toenails painted to match fingernails) were bound in slender thongs of gold-embossed leather far too elegant to be called sandals. And their faces . . . oh, I couldn't take my eyes away from their faces! Their skin was pale, pale olive with a pearly sheen on it, and their eyes were enormous: brown and almond-shaped and fringed by long, thick lashes. I wanted nothing more than simply to stare and stare at them. I loved them both on sight. This was not at all surprising. What is much harder to understand is why they were so interested in me, and so nice to me, and why they decided that for the duration of my holiday, I was to be a combination of little sister, mascot and doll to play with.

They used to spend whole afternoons dressing me up, letting me try on all their clothes and perfumes. They gossiped in front of me, exotic tales of infidelity and betrayal about people I'd always thought of as boring and staid. They confided their dreams and dearest wishes. They taught me songs in French, and played records for me on their portable record-player. They let me have small sips of alcoholic drinks from their glasses, and they let me go everywhere with them: shopping, to the hairdresser's, and to the beach. Whenever there was a dance at the club, they took endless trouble arranging my hair, drawing lines around my eyes, doing what they could with what was rather unpromising raw material. Leila and Yasmina insisted I was an 'English Rose', but they were much given to exaggeration. I had long, blonde hair, neatly plaited most of the time, wishy-washy blue eyes and a fair complexion.

'Let me finish this hairdo,' Leila said to my reflection in the glass, 'and then I will shout at Yasmina.'

'There's nothing to shout about,' said Yasmina. 'It's true. Marc is coming back from Dakar today, and you are restless. Not,' she continued, taking another square of Turkish delight from the dish on the bedside table, 'that I can blame you. He is so handsome. Pat, don't you think he's the most handsome creature you've ever seen? And he is French . . . so glamorous . . .'

'Jolly handsome,' I said. 'And he's a man.'

Leila and Yasmina laughed.

'What else should he be?' asked Yasmina. 'A giraffe?'

'Silly!' I said, also giggling. 'You know what I mean. He's not a boy, that's all. I mean he's grown up. He's a friend of my parents'. He's had dinner in our house lots of times, and it's hard not to think of him as old. I mean, he *is* twenty-eight, after all.'

This remark of mine convulsed them. Leila fell back on to the bed where Yasmina was already reclining, and they rolled around, their pearls of laughter twinkling and sparkling up towards the ceiling where the three-bladed fan was stirring the warm, heavy air of the afternoon.

'Old!' Leila wiped the tears from her eyes. 'My child, haven't I told you how smooth the skin is on his back? How strong he is?'

'How he nibbles you all over,' Yasmina added, shrieking with merriment, 'with his white, white teeth . . . which are all his own. Not false teeth, I assure you!'

I blushed. I used to find the way the sisters spoke so openly about such physical matters dreadfully embarrassing at first, but I was getting used to it, little by little. Leila and Yasmina had made me bolder. There would even come a day, I supposed, when my speech would be as sprinkled with innuendo as theirs was. For the moment, I still squirmed a bit, privately, but I only said, 'Leila, he's lovely. Everyone is frightfully envious. I know I am.'

'You, my little baby sister,' said Leila, 'are exactly half his age. You must wait for such treats.'

My father drove me to the club for the dance, through the streets of the town, where white buildings were hung with trailing bougainvillaeas in shades of magenta and scarlet, and then along the coast road, through a landscape vibrating with green: the grasses and creepers and palm trees on one side, and the turquoise and malachite ocean on the other.

'You don't have to wait for me,' I said. 'There are tons of people who can drive me home. I can come back with Leila and Marc. He's not a teenager. He's properly grown up.'

My father sniffed. 'They'll all be as drunk as Bandusian goats. I shall read the magazines in the reading room as usual.'

I had no idea what a Bandusian goat was. The expression was one my father often used. I knew he would be quite happy reading back numbers of *Punch* and *The Illustrated London News* and chatting to whoever else was in the reading room until I was ready to leave.

Leila and Yasmina were at the club when I arrived, but there was no sign of Marc. Leila was wearing a shiny cherry-red dress, with a full skirt puffed out by layer upon layer of stiff net petticoats in sweet-pea colours. A gold belt around her waist caught the light, and gold bangles slid musically up and down her arm as she moved.

'Gosh,' I said. 'You look gorgeous. And so do you, Yasmina.'

'I am being self-effacing tonight,' said Yasmina, 'not wishing to eclipse my sister!' She smiled. If her mauve satin blouse was supposed to be self-effacing, I dreaded to think what would happen when Yasmina wanted to make an emphatic statement.

'Where's Marc?' I asked. 'I thought he'd be with you.'

'He telephoned me,' said Leila. She seemed distracted, as if her mind were on something else. 'He said there was someone he wanted me to meet. A surprise, he said.'

Until Marc arrived, Leila and Yasmina danced with other young men. I watched them closely, even when I was dancing myself. Amidst the pallid floral prints and pastel colours of the ladies of Bathurst, their jewel colours glowed and shimmered. Next to the leathery brown or lobster pink of bare colonial arms and shoulders, their flesh was like ivory.

When Marc came in with a woman, I looked at Leila and saw her flinch. A tremor ran through her body, and she looked all at once like a deer, struck through the heart by an arrow. There was a flurry of introductions. The woman was called Chantal. Marc had known her since childhood. She was tall, almost as tall as Marc, pale-skinned, red-headed, dressed in something that was so chic as to be virtually invisible: a sheath of brown linen. I hated her at once, but she was beautiful. Different from Leila, but lovely: a lily where Leila was a rose.

The music went on and on. Leila and Marc were dancing. Yasmina was also dancing, but steering her partner closer to her sister, probably to try and catch something of Marc's unceasing stream of talk. He was clearly saying something urgent, important, and Leila was saying nothing at all. Round and round went the music and round and round went the dancers, and I looked at Leila and felt in my heart that her heart was bleeding. The evening continued.

'If it was me,' I said to Yasmina, 'I would leave. Why doesn't she leave?'

'And give that woman the satisfaction of knowing that she has hurt her? Never.' Yasmina shook her head. 'In any case, until I speak to Leila, I don't know what he has said, or who this person is. I shall wait and see.'

It was nearly eleven o'clock when Marc asked me to dance. I didn't know how to refuse, so I accepted. I couldn't think of anything to say to him, so I said nothing.

'You are quiet tonight,' he said at last. 'I was expecting to hear all the latest gossip, the latest news, but no luck . . .'

'There's no news,' I said.

'You are angry with me, *ma petite*,' he said, 'and I would like to know what I have done to you to make in you this anger.'

'You haven't done anything to *me*,' I said, laying heavy emphasis on 'me'. 'It's Leila. It's what you've done to her.' It crossed my mind as I spoke that it was none of my business, that I was only a child and perhaps I shouldn't be speaking like this to someone twice my age.

'Oh, *là là*,' Marc said. '*Qu'est-ce que vous voulez, les femmes*? What do you want of a man? Did I make Leila any promise? Does she own me? Did she seriously think . . .' He broke off.

'Think what?' I asked.

'That I would be willing to marry her?' Marc frowned.

'She never spoke of marriage,' I said. 'But she loves you.'

'And I also think she is lovely,' Marc said. The music turned and turned and we turned with it.

I said, 'But you don't love her.'

Marc shrugged his shoulders. 'Oh, *ça, alors . . .*' he said, and that was all he said, but I understood instantly. It was as though a kaleidoscope had twisted, and all at once fallen into a pattern of unspeakable ugliness. I knew. I knew exactly what he meant. He could never love Leila, never marry Leila, never, because she was Syrian. An Arab. Different. Not French, and therefore slightly inferior. Not, as I had once heard someone say, 'one of us'.

At the end of the dance, I said to Marc, 'I don't feel very well. I'm going to find my father.'

I was too sick at heart even to speak to Leila. I glanced over to the bar, and there she was with Yasmina, laughing, with a drink in her hand. I thought: how brave she is! I shall go and visit her tomorrow. We will eat sugared almonds. I shall comfort her.

I left the room and went to find my father. He was surprised that I wanted to leave so early.

Mrs Mahdi telephoned my mother the next

morning. She could hardly speak for crying. Leila and Yasmina's car had crashed into a tree on the way home from the club. Yasmina would be allowed home in a day or two, but Leila was badly injured. She would have to stay in hospital for some time.

The following week, I visited Yasmina at the Mahdis' house and, a few days after that, she took me with her to visit Leila in hospital. I'd been dreaming about how she would look, imagining her encased in plaster with only her bloodstained face showing. I dreaded seeing her and was longing to see her at the same time. Would she be able to speak? What would I say? I couldn't think of anything at all.

I don't like hospitals. I hate the smell, and the silence and the occasional terrible sight you just glimpse out of the corner of your eye as you walk down the ward. I followed Yasmina, staring at the back of her neck so as to see no unexpected horrors. I was plucking up courage to look at Leila.

'Oh,' I said when I saw her. 'You look just the same! I thought you'd be wrapped in bandages. Can you talk? Are you . . . how do you feel?'

'Stitched together.' Leila smiled faintly. 'They brought their needles and they sewed and sewed, and here under the sheet, that is where the bandages begin. I am empty. I feel . . . there is nothing inside.' She tapped her breast. 'No more heart.'

'But, Leila, think!' I burst out. 'You could, you might have been killed. Imagine that.'

She answered only: 'Yes . . .' but the word stretched out and filled the space around us, like a sigh. There was a look in her eyes that I didn't understand then.

Word in the Colony was that the road was slippery, and that the corner where the Mahdi sisters had crashed was notoriously difficult, and that Leila had maybe had a little too much to drink. I believed it too, at the time, but now I think Leila wanted to die. The look on her face in the hospital ... I realise now what it was. It was a longing, a desire for death. Leila had simply wanted not to be. Thirty-five years after the event, I understand.

The Facts of Life
ALICK ROWE

'Sex, sex, sex,' Bernice Winters snapped. 'That's all your generation thinks about. You may fool your father but you don't fool me.' Stuart shut the car door.

'Thanks for the lift, Mum,' he said, pulling his collar up against the drizzle and running for the school gates.

'Sex?' Julie's father looked up from his computer screen. Julie sighed and reached for her briefcase.

'Sniggering boys and giggling girls. Really boring,' she said, giving his beard a friendly tug and kissing him goodbye.

'Sex lessons!' whooped Ted. 'Brilliant!' He whooped again and clanged his locker shut, grinning round at the rest of the boys. He wiped his glasses which were steaming up.

'In this first session,' smiled Miss Clarke to the hushed biology room, 'Mr Pulver and I are going to talk about problems of adolescence.'

Mr Pulver stepped forward. 'The important thing is to be honest,' he said, 'not embarrassed. These things have happened to everybody – me, Miss Clarke, your parents, the headmaster.' The group shifted anxiously.

(Idiot! thought Sara. Don't scare them to death.) She broke in, smiling, 'The point is, nobody knows it all but too many people think they do.' She pointed at a boy in the front row. 'How much about the subject do *you* know?'

The boy stood. 'Nothing. I don't know anything about . . . all that.'

Jeering swirled round the room. 'Dickhead!' called Ted and girls giggled but Sara Clarke raised a hand for silence. She rather admired his bravery. So did Julie.

'What's your name?'

'Stuart Winters.' He smiled. It was a strange beam that suddenly switched on and just as suddenly off. Julie found herself smiling in response. So did Miss Clarke.

The session was an anticlimax. They had looked forward to forbidden fruit but found themselves discussing things they always talked about anyway – shyness, hygiene, moods, freedom – and when the bell rang they filed out with familiar weariness. Stuart and Julie came face to face in the crowded doorway. Stuart nodded, Julie smiled shyly and they walked politely side by side towards the junction of the corridors.

'What class are you in?' he asked.

'3C.'

'I'm in 3N. Stuart Winters. What's your name?'

'Julie Griffiths.' She peeled off to her classroom. 'See you, Stuart.'

'See you, Julie,' he called back.

Locker-room opinion was unanimous about the dismal beginning to the sex season. 'Megaboring!' chanted Ted. He hurried after his departing friends. 'What d'you think of the Clarke tart then?'

he panted. 'Pulver's got the hots for her, if you ask me.' He cleaned his glasses on his tie. He was getting steamed up again.

Her father handed her the pasta salad. 'So how was it?'

'I met a boy,' she replied. Her father was so careful not to react that she knew he was surprised.

Graham, her brother, looked up. 'Who?'

She reached for the pitta bread. 'Stuart Winters, 3N.'

Graham had his mouth full. 'Don't know him,' he spattered.

'Careful, son,' murmured Felix, wiping sauce from his beard. 'Go carefully, Both of you.'

'S.E.X!!!' wrote Ted in his diary. 'With Pathetic Pulver and Sarky Clarky!!!' He crossed out 'Sarky' and substituted 'Tarty'. He underlined 'Tarty'. He drew a mountainous pair of breasts and coloured the nipples red. He added a final exclamation mark and hid the diary away.

Bernard Winters looked solemnly at his son, propped up on his pillows. 'And that is *exactly* how the lesson went?' He looked solemnly at his wife who solemnly looked back at him. Stuart felt the air was electric with secret signals. Then they bowed heads and closed their eyes.

'God keep this family safe from sin, loving and ever vigilant.' They murmured, 'Amen,' and moved on to the Lord's Prayer.

The following Thursday, Lesson Two – Health for the Growing Teenager – was no improvement. Miss Clarke dealt with food and nutrition – just because she happens to be a woman, Julie guessed – after which Brian Pulver slumped lazily forward to switch on the video about posture, exercise and sleep. Stuart noticed that Miss Clarke kept her nicotine-stained fingers behind her back during the discussion on smoking and the final topic of the session was the importance of keeping clean.

'Sweat glands under the arm,' said Miss Clarke, 'can make people sweat heavily if they're excited or nervous.'

'Hello, Linda,' Ted called quietly.

'And without regular washing, the resulting bacteria can cause unpleasant smells.'

'Hello, Donald,' Ted called less quietly.

Sara Clarke pressed on. 'Bacteria also causes tooth decay but regular brushing will help check this. So will eating fewer sweet things. Tooth decay may lead to halitosis – otherwise known as bad breath.'

'Hello, Janet,' Ted called.

Sara Clarke paused. 'Acne, on the other hand,' she said, 'is caused less by bacteria than changes in hormones – particularly the male one: testosterone – which is why boys are spottier than girls.'

'Hello, Ted,' yelled everybody in the room. Neither teacher tried to stop the laughter.

Stuart and Julie walked up the corridor side by side.

'I live in Elm Court Road,' he offered. 'What about you?'

Julie looked across at him. 'Quarry Avenue,' she said.

'Gross! Gross!' complained Ted, stamping past, clearly shaken by the lesson. 'That was disgusting!'

They grinned and walked on. They would have

liked to talk more but the lesson had spoiled the mood. Stuart secretly agreed with Ted: it had been gross. He bet Julie thought so too.

'Puberty begins in the brain,' said Sara Clarke. 'This is the hypothalamus.' She pointed to a green nodule dangling beneath a big blue brain. As the group stared at the diagrams of the two figures and inwardly yawned Stuart wished he was brave enough to move towards Julie at his side. 'The hypothalamus sends hormones to the pituitary gland –' she tapped a yellowish streak – 'which triggers the release of hormones called FSH and LH.' Julie cunningly edged closer to Stuart. 'They develop eggs in the girls' ovaries – here.' Sara Clarke pointed at two yellow circles situated vaguely below the waist of the right-hand figure. 'And sperm in the boys' testes – here.' She smartly tapped two similar circles vaguely below the waist of its neighbour and Julie felt Stuart wince. The slide changed and there was a silent gasp as a naked teenage boy and girl smiled from the screen. Brian Pulver stepped forward.

'The first thing you may notice,' he said – automatically using the silly voice he used when embarrassed and immediately correcting it – 'the first thing you may notice,' he intoned solemnly, 'is hair.'

Wrong, thought Stuart, fascinated by the girl's breasts. He rested his left thigh very gently against Julie Griffiths' right thigh, scared of her reaction and relieved when she moved her hand so that their little fingers were touching on the table.

Mr Pulver was the hair expert – pubic hair, hair under the arms, hair on the face, stray hairs anywhere – but there was a limit to its fascination and Sara Clarke stepped forward.

'Breasts,' she said firmly.

Stuart gaped at the textbook diagram, deeply impressed by Miss Clarke's explanation of how a female body produces milk. He edged his leg and finger from contact; somehow it didn't seem right to feel sexy about the owner of two such serious inventions. Miss Clarke was handing leaflets to the girls about buying a bra, talking about breast sizes, and Stuart yearned to look at Julie's breasts but didn't dare. Slyly he moved his leg back into contact.

A massive diagram of the male sex organs flashed on the screen and Stuart felt Julie pull away. Brian Pulver gingerly approached the screen with his pointer to take the class on what he described as a quick guided tour. The temptation to slip into his silly voice was almost irresistible.

Julie sneaked a sideways look at Stuart and felt sorry for him. As Mr Pulver prodded the prostate gland she moved so they were touching again and they were busy entwining little fingers when the male sex organs were replaced by the female.

Stuart's mouth gaped even wider. The diagram looked like nothing he had ever imagined. Julie glared blankly at the screen. That has nothing to do with me, she thought. It looked like a bicycle saddle. There was relief all round when Miss Clarke released the boys early so that she could talk privately to the girls about their periods.

'I'll wait for you,' Stuart whispered as he gathered his books.

Julie shook her head. 'See you tonight. The usual place.' Stuart smiled widely and left.

Her father's unasked questions hung heavily in the

air as Julie chopped artichokes for pizza.

'Hormones, hair, breasts, genitals and periods,' she said at last. 'Shall I grate the cheese?'

Felix Griffiths tossed the dough. 'Why don't you bring Stuart home tonight?' he asked.

'It's OK, thanks,' she quickly replied, hearing Graham slam the back door.

'It was just a lot of talk, Dad,' Stuart said. 'FSH, LH, pituitary glands. Mr Pulver told us about shaving.'

The secret signals flew but Bernard Winters eventually bowed his head. 'God keep this family safe from sin, loving and ever vigilant.'

Halfway through the Lord's Prayer Stuart remembered kissing Julie two hours ago and touching her breasts through her kaftan. He opened his eyes to find his mother staring suspiciously at him and immediately slammed them shut.

For the fourth session of the course they were joined by a round, twinkling-eyed man in middle age. Sara Clarke stepped forward. 'This is Dr Andrews.'

Dr Andrews took off his jacket. 'Love,' he said slowly, as if hearing the word for the first time. 'Love,' he repeated, tasting it like wine. 'Love,' he concluded, shaking his head in wonder. He pointed round the room. 'There are people in this room who are in love.' He smiled warmly. 'I can tell.' He closed his eyes as if overcome at the idea.

The class was riveted. There wasn't a sound.

Dr Andrews walked up and down the room. 'Love makes the world go round,' he said chattily to goggle-eyed Ted. 'All you need is love,' he sang to Anne who blushed. Dr Andrews turned to everyone. 'Love is the greatest emotion!' He looked into their wide eyes. 'So let's try to understand it.'

Twenty minutes later they were all experts. Even 3N's macho element, usually so aggressive towards homosexuality, meekly accepted that strong feelings for the same sex were possible.

'How many people in this room?' smiled Dr Andrews. 'Thirty? Then at least three of us will live a gay life-style and good luck to them.' Everyone took care not to look at Frank while Stuart wondered who the other two might be, unaware of Susan and Christine holding hands in the corner near the door.

'Perfect love casts out fear.' Like all his sayings, it was true. Dr Andrews was such a wise man. Stuart and Julie longed for the lights to go down.

At the end of the session the group was unusually quiet. Julie and Stuart walked together but there seemed nothing to say. Dr Andrews had said it all for them.

'See you tonight,' he whispered at the parting of the ways. 'I love you.'

'I love you too,' she replied.

Dr Andrews winked at Miss Clarke, outside the biology room, the following Thursday, and the general feeling was that the Big Day was here at last.

Generally, they were not disappointed. There was no real-life video of love-making, as Ted had hoped, but there were full diagrams, photographs of microscope slides and detailed line drawings. The session was embarrassing enough for those who wished to be embarrassed and sexy enough for those who wished to be turned on. For those who wished to learn, it was informative.

Three hundred million. Julie's head simply refused to get round the extraordinary sum. Three hundred million sperms every time. She gazed at Stuart with new respect and wondered how anybody had counted them.

'But of course,' continued Dr Andrews, 'only a thousand get as far as the uterine tubes before they die.'

Only a thousand? thought Stuart, alarmed at the thought of this wriggly horde stampeding through Julie's womb like lemmings.

They watched a successful sperm join with an ovum whose cell divided until it became a cluster. 'This happens between one week and ten days after intercourse and the moment it has implanted itself the woman is pregnant.' Dr Andrews looked triumphantly round and Stuart and Julie just had time to move apart before the lights switched on. They glanced at each other with shining eyes, exhausted by the process of love-making. It was their finest hour.

Graham looked round Julie's door on his way from the shower. 'I know who your boyfriend is,' he called, padding along the landing. 'Better not let Dad find out.'

Stuart hated lying.

'Where were you tonight, son?' Bernard Winters persisted.

'Nowhere,' Stuart mumbled and turned away only to meet his mother's accusing gaze.

'What have you been up to?' she asked.

Stuart stared down at the duvet. 'Nothing,' he insisted. Signals flew and it seemed ages before his father bowed his head for family prayers.

'Whatever's the matter?' cried Ted's mother, snapping on his light. Ted gazed wildly around the room from a sweaty tangle of sheets.

His father hurried in. 'What's up, lad?' he asked. 'Nightmare?'

Ted nodded, appalled.

The sixth session enchanted them both. Stuart and Julie held hands openly now, an acknowledged couple, and when the lights went down Julie slipped her right hand into the back pocket of Stuart's jeans and he slipped a respectful arm round her waist. They thrilled to see last week's cluster of cells survive twelve weeks into a recognisable human. Amazing film techniques enabled everyone to see the growth of the baby inside the womb.

'After six months,' smiled Dr Andrews, 'our baby –' Stuart and Julie beamed at each other – 'can probably hear voices, music and other sounds above the steady beat of Mother's heart. Soon Baby's kicks can be felt by laying a hand on Mother's tummy.' He smiled while Miss Clarke remembered only fatigue, constipation, depression, backache and feeling sick.

There was some apprehension among the girls at the size to which Baby developed – 'God almighty!' whispered Donna – but Dr Andrews reassuringly explained the expansion of the pelvis and birth canal. They watched a video on Dangers to the Unborn Baby and when the lights went up Stuart and Julie made hardly any attempt to move apart. They felt that the baby whose progress they had been following had become their own. They were full of hope and feeling very mature.

* * *

Stuart carried her heavy briefcase along the corridor. 'I've got to see you tonight,' he whispered.

Julie looked round to check that nobody was listening. 'All right,' she said slowly, 'only . . .'

Stuart glanced across. 'Only what?'

Julie smiled. 'Nothing,' she murmured. 'I love you.' She quickly kissed his cheek, took her briefcase and ran towards her classroom.

'God, you two make me sick, sick, sick!' shouted Ted as he passed.

'S.E.X!!!' wrote Ted. 'Winters and Griffiths are DOING IT!! DISGUSTING REVOLTING!!!' He quickly sketched his impression of Stuart and Julie doing it in a forest of exclamation marks. He underlined REVOLTING and DISGUSTING and was about to draw something else revolting and disgusting when he heard steps on the stairs and slipped the diary into hiding.

It had taken seven weeks to arrive at the Miracle of Birth. The breathless group watched a graphic video charting events from the moment parents arrived at hospital until the successful delivery of Baby. It was extraordinarily powerful to follow the emergence of a new human being. Stuart and Julie even forgot to hold hands as they watched Reassuring Father massage Anxious Mother.

Miss Clarke snorted bitterly. (Chance would have been a fine thing, she recalled and was suddenly aware that Dr Andrews was holding her hand.)

Mother was monitored and her contractions eased by inhaling gas and air. It was so dramatic – even when Mr Pulver hurriedly left the room at a close-up of Mother's painkilling injection, hardly anybody noticed. The tension in the room grew electric as the Moment approached and when Baby finally slipped from Mother into Nurse's hands there was a widespread gasp and Stuart and Julie kissed each other in the dark. Ted fainted when Nurse clamped and cut the umbilical cord but that was the last distraction. It was a girl. Just what Stuart wanted; Julie would have preferred a boy. They had decided on names the night before: Zoë.

After Ted's departure with Dr Andrews the group learned about multiple births, breech births and caesarean births, but the show was really over the moment little Zoë took centre stage with her dark blue eyes and downy head of hair.

Sara Clarke watched Julie and Stuart drift from the room hand in hand, the last to leave. She was on the point of calling out something amusing or ironic but suddenly felt a lump in her throat. She smiled at Dr Andrews as Brian Pulver folded away the screen.

'Julie?'

She already had a hand on the front door but turned and looked into the study where Felix was tapping at his keyboard.

'What is it?' she asked.

Her father stared at the screen. 'I don't want you out tonight.' There was silence as the mood turned dangerous. His hands dropped and he raised his eyes. 'You didn't tell me who Stuart's father is.'

Julie swivelled angrily to Graham, reading in a corner, refusing to meet her glance, and six seconds later she was in the street striding to Elm Court Road.

Bernard and Bernice Winters waited for Stuart to return. On the table lay his Thursday notes, the textbook and a drawing that Ted had stuffed between the pages just to show to knew what was happening between Stuart and Julie. Bernice Winters' closed eyes suggested that she was praying while her husband, Pastor of the New Church Of Jesus, wrote angrily to the headmaster of his son's school about betrayal and corruption.

At the beginning of the final Thursday session, Mr Pulver announced that Dr Andrews had been called away for important research, though few of the group were fooled: the story of Sara Clarke's struggle in the equipment room against the doctor's ardent advances was widely reported and they looked at her through new eyes. It was better gossip than Stuart Winters' removal from school by his nutty father and, as Brian Pulver droned on about unwanted babies, contraception, failure rates, AIDS and abortion, Julie sat in silent misery, not really listening, just thinking numbly that it was all over: the end of the affair.

It had started so well all those weeks ago – getting to know each other, exploring feelings, learning about their bodies, being responsible. She remembered the birth of little Zoë and tears gathered in her eyes. She remembered last Thursday night – they had guessed it would be their last meeting – and the tears eased down to her cheeks. Her hand automatically moved to her stomach where – according to Dr Andrews – it would be almost six months before Baby could begin to hear music and voices above the firm solid beat of Mother's heart.

'Fancy a quick drink in the Kestrel?' asked Brian, stacking books in the staffroom cupboard.

'OK,' Sara agreed. She was dying for a fag anyway.

'We might go for a curry afterwards,' he suggested licking his lips. He too was finding Miss Clarke suddenly more interesting.

'S.E.X!!!' Ted wrote. 'Scandal. Doc. Andrews rapped –' his spelling was none too good – 'Tarty Clarky in the book room. Boohoo Pulver!!! Winters expelled for doing it to Griffiths. SERVES –' he underlined it once – 'THEM –' he underlined it twice – 'RIGHT.' He underlined the last word three times and surrounded the whole entry with more exclamation marks before shutting the cover, locking the clasp, concealing the diary in its secret place, hiding the key, and trying hard not to meet the beady accusing eyes of his threadbare old teddy glittering down at him from a shelf.

The Women's Hour
ROBERT WESTALL

I think I was a pretty child; though I have never been pretty since. My photographs show solemn dark eyes, silky black hair, a smooth skin. Perhaps that was why they always wanted to kiss me.

Or perhaps women kissed more then. Nothing sexy about it; just great big hugs and smacking kisses, for nearly everybody. And the little fishing harbour where I lived as a child seemed full of women. Aunties and honorary aunties, friends of my mother. For a long time I couldn't tell the difference. Big-bodied warm women, in faded floral pinnies. Aunt Rosie, Aunt Nellie, Aunt Bessie, Aunt Maggie, Aunt Laura. Who picked me up like I was a parcel and kissed me without as much as a by-your-leave. The sea of aunties stretched away to the expanding fringes of my world. Once, aged four, I ventured far too far and got lost. I was whipped up the moment I started to cry by a totally strange aunty, who not only kissed me but took me home, gave me first sweets and then drinks and, once she could get a word of sense out of me, carried me all the way home to my mother, who embraced her in turn. Every street was safe, because it had an aunty in it, cleaning her windows or polishing her already gleaming knocker.

Even the men kissed me. I liked this less. Men

had harder hands, they smelt of tobacco or worse, beer, and their faces had the consistency of sandpaper. Worst was my grandfather, who had a Kaiser Bill moustache that felt like a scrubbing-brush. How utterly *unnatural*, to have a scrubbing-brush forever attached to your face. Actually, my grandfather was the first casualty, the first I dared show reluctance about. I suppose I sensed a reluctance in him too. There was a stiff darkness in my grandfather; he had spent four years in the trenches, and drank too much to forget. Anyway, we were soon subjected to a shared female blackmail.

'Haven't you got a kiss for your poor old granda?'

'Give the bairn a kiss, Bob, it's not natural . . .'

My father was the next to get rejected. Coming straight from the engine-room of a trawler, he smelt of coal, soot, oil and other unromantic things. His sooty cheek *tasted* of oil, too.

But unlike the men, the women would not be put off by my unwillingness. They made their demands, and waited confidently till they were met. Even the old ladies with warts on their faces, from which grey hairs straggled. Agony, to be performed with my eyes tight shut, under the scrutiny of a dozen pairs of female eyes. I often worried that I was unnatural. I mean I used to hear of other children who liked nothing better than going to bed with their grandfather for a nap every afternoon . . .

The only person I could bear to be cuddled by for long was my mother, and if she held me too tight, I would push away, shouting, 'Don't struggle me, don't struggle me.'

The termly nit inspections at school, when the district nurse, Nitty Norah, grabbed you by the ears and buried your face chokingly into her enormous bosom came near to putting me off women for life.

Relief seemed to come with the war, when I was nine. Suddenly I became as busy and military as a soldier. Even for the aunts, big cuddles turned into swift pecks on the cheeks. Mind you, I noticed that the general level of kissing didn't go down much, if at all. Our little railway station, on a Friday night, with the men coming home on leave . . . but this was sexy kissing for the first time in public. Couples running at each other from hundreds of yards away, as the trains came in. Flinging themselves, burying themselves into each other, while the man's kitbags fell off his shoulders and rolled about the platform, even on to the railway lines. And the girls had this trick of throwing one nylon-clad leg into the air behind them to show the extent of their love. One respectable married woman, whose husband was soon to go into the RAF took to kissing him passionately on the doorstep every morning before work. This, the other mothers did not approve of. Best kept for the bedroom, our mothers muttered, and nearly ostracised her as if she was some sort of tart . . .

But there was no stopping it, even in the bosom of the family. When my cousin Charlie came home on leave, he and his fiancée took up permanent residence on the couch, coiled in a heap, muttering and giggling and kissing even when the whole family was sat there, and not a word of sense could anyone get out of them. I couldn't bear to look.

And in the fields . . . I became most reluctant to go up to the farm for a gill of milk after dark. When I joined the Boy Scouts in 1942, nobody said that bit about Scouts being clean in thought, word and deed more fervently than me.

But soon after that, a weariness seemed to descend on our harbour, and mostly among the women. I mean, my father was *spectacularly* tired. Life had always been hard for the trawlermen. They'd always had to snatch sleep when they could, with shooting the nets in the middle of the night, and getting wet through three or four times a trip and not eating properly. But now they had worse things to contend with; deadly magnetic mines dragged up in their nets, and Junkers bombers machine-gunning them in broad daylight, and them with only a single Lewis gun to defend themselves with. Often my Dad came home too tired to even eat. Just stretched out and was snoring on our sofa, in all his dirty gear.

So I hardly noticed how tired my Mam was getting. She was always very pale now. And often she sat my father and me down to a good fried meal, but said she didn't feel hungry, would only have a little brown bread and butter. Looking back I realise she was half-starving herself to feed us. She seemed to have no energy. And all the women looked the same, old headscarves and backs bent over shopping bags.

D-Day seemed to put more life back into the men, in a bitter way. They talked about the end now, and Jerry getting what he deserved, and what they would like to do with Hitler. But I found my mother crying when I got home after school on D-Day, cock-a-hoop and avid for the six o'clock news. I told her she was being stupid, it was a *marvellous* day. But she said she was crying for all the mother's sons who were dying . . .

It came home two weeks later. The girl who lived next door to us had a telegram. Her husband had been shot down and killed in the RAF; an air-gunner he was. They'd been married just two months; we'd all gone to the wedding, and they'd been so happy and so much in love. She was only eighteen, and we'd kept an eye on her, because she had no family of her own. She was often round our house for a meal. She was a pretty, curvy, blonde little thing, so full of life and so proud of her husband.

My mother spent two days round there, with her. We hardly saw her. And other women kept going in and out of the house all the time, with little wartime titbits, to tempt her to eat. But my Mam said she wouldn't touch a thing; only drink glasses of water.

I kept well out of the way; scurried past her door in case she came out. I couldn't bear it. So when my Mam said, about a month later, 'Why don't you drop in to see Margie? It'd be a bit of company for her. A bit of young life. She must get tired of all us old crows flapping round her,' I got into a total panic, and refused flat. And I would have gone on refusing flat, if I hadn't been in our garden, cleaning out my rabbits, when she came out into hers, to hang out a few poor bits of female washing. I was bent down behind the hutches, so she didn't see me. But I watched her, fascinated and horrified.

But she just looked the same old Margie. They'd said she'd lost a terrible lot of weight, with grieving. But she didn't look any thinner to me. Perhaps she'd started eating again by that time. Her hair was lank and greasy, and her frock had some splashes down the front, that was all. Her cat came home then, and she began talking to it, just like she always had. And I realised I'd been a total fool, scaring myself sick about her. Because I'd been a bit keen on Margie, in my fourteen-year-old way. I mean, just watching her when she came to our house, and showing her the best guns in my model army.

So I stood up, and said, 'Hallo, Margie!' and she gave a jump and clutched at her throat, and said, 'Oh, Ben! You didn't half give me a fright jumping up like that. Like a jack-in-the-box.' And we both laughed a bit, and she said, 'It must be hot work doing out them rabbits. Would you like a glass of lemonade?' And I was so keen to make it up to her, that I climbed over her fence without going round to the front gate, and tore the crotch of my trousers a bit, but I hoped she wouldn't notice.

We sat in her little parlour, with the big photo of her husband in his RAF uniform watching us, all Brylcreem and sadness, from the sideboard. My eyes would not stay away from it, as I sipped my lemonade; it had me transfixed, like a stoat does to a rabbit.

She saw me looking, and she said, 'It's a funny old life, Ben. Some of the girls I went to school with are still in the sixth form. I'd have been there myself, mebbe, if I hadn't met Tom and got married. And now I'm an old widow-woman.'

She cried a bit then, but very quietly, just the tears running down her face and nose and chin, and splashing into the lap of her old frock. She said suddenly, frightened, 'Oh, I am stupid. I'm scaring you away. Sorry. *Sorry.*'

But I said, quite firmly, 'You won't scare *me* away.' And reached out and took her hand off her lap, and held it, till she'd stopped crying.

Then she said, again, 'Sorry,' and dried her eyes on a rather dirty hanky, and said, 'Tell me all the village gossip. I've hardly been out of doors.'

So I prattled on, about harmless things, like old Billie Toshack, the air-raid warden, who still went round shouting, 'Put that light out,' though there hadn't been an air-raid for two years. And the whale meat we'd been having, that tasted of fish till you soaked it for twenty-four hours in vinegar, after which it just tasted like vinegar. And that joke about Vera Lynn singing her song 'Whale Meat again'. I had her laughing in the end.

Then she said, 'Would you like me to cook you some chips?' though it was only three in the afternoon, and I said, 'Yeah, please.'

After that, I called in about three times a week, and I hope I did her some good. It wasn't hard work. She would cry a bit most times, but softly, and I just held her hand till she stopped, and it was nice.

Well, winter passed, a hard hungry weary winter. And then it was spring. And I noticed a change in the women. I mean, all the men could talk about was the advance on the Rhine, and the Americans hammering the Japs in the Pacific. But the women seemed to have a new spring in their step. I began to hear the word 'celebrations'. Mrs Pym, the vicar's wife, got the Mothers' Union to root in the church hall, under the stage, and they discovered, covered with dust, all the stuff from the 1936 Coronation Tea, which we'd held on the village green, at the top end by the church, on the cliff above the harbour. One Monday morning, every washing-line seemed to carry a large Union Jack and endless yards of bunting. And Miss Martineau, the schoolmistress began to rehearse mysterious dancing and pageants about St George.

My Mam seemed more concerned about how you could make decent sandwiches with national wholemeal bread, which just crumbled when you tried to slice it. And there was a lot of coaxing of grocers, and bags of flour began to build up in our larder, and there were trips to the farms, to coax eggs out of the farmers' wives. Everywhere you looked, there were women plotting in little groups.

Of course, people think now that Mr Churchill just suddenly announced the end of the war, and the whole nation spontaneously went mad. But in reality, we could see it coming a mile off. In the newspapers, the maps of Germany were so full of the arrows of advancing armies there wasn't any room left for any Germans. Jeff Lott said he'd give more chance to a broken fishbox on our stormy rocks than he would to Hitler now. So when the announcement came, we were ready down to the last trestle table and cup.

That day, I flung myself into things. Men were scarce. Half of them were away at the war, and most of what was left were kids and doddery old gaffers who couldn't lift a tea urn, though my Granda, who was handy with his hands like my dad, was a great help putting up the hired loudspeakers and gramophone. And Billy Sims, he'd got a scratch band together for the dancing. Violin, squeezebox and piano. And an able seaman on leave turned up with a saxophone. He was the only one in the band under sixty. And all the kids in the neighbourhood lent an enthusiastic hand with the huge bonfire they were building. There were so many wooden things we didn't need any more, like the bunk beds from the air-raid shelters, and signs saying 'Warden's Post'.

But it was the women who were so amazing. Working non-stop, gassing non-stop, flinging their hair around loose, with all headscarves gone.

Throwing back their heads and laughing, enjoying exposing their throats to the sun. They didn't walk, they *danced*. I've seen it since many times at weddings, that dancing female step, that wanting to touch everything, that excited laughter. Every time a woman gets married, it's as if all her friends, married and single, are getting married with her. Whereas the men stand extra-stolidly, and drink and mutter, or fiddle with their big cameras and video recorders so solemnly. Why don't men join in rejoicing? What were they *afraid* of? If they hadn't been afraid of Junkers bombers and Hitler . . .

I mean, when my mother learnt that our little fleet was going out fishing as usual that night . . . there was a real row, I can tell you. My father muttered about making the most of a sea full of fish and empty of Jerries, but . . .

Well, the day passed. The schoolkids stumbled through their tribute to St George, with loud embarrassed shouting voices. The girls danced beautifully, the boys resentfully. 'God Save the King' seemed to alternate with 'The White Cliffs of Dover' all day. And then it was time for the younger kids, full to the gills with seven different recipes for artificial cream (one said to include hair oil), to be pushed off to bed or at least to be sick privately down the toilet.

It started again around dusk, round the bonfire on the cliff-top. The fishing fleet had gone, my mother calling after my father, in a taunting voice, 'Spoilsport.' It was then, as the band struck up, that I realised how many women there were, and how few men. And what men there were were mostly old gaffers watching from chairs that had been brought out for them. All those still hale and hearty seemed to be in the band, or fiddling with the loudspeakers, or gone off to the pub. There were just three young soldiers in uniform.

But the women were not deterred, as the flames shot higher and higher, and darkness fell, and the band went into an eight-some reel. The three young soldiers, protesting half-heartedly, were snatched up. And then I, just turned fifteen, and not even realising till then that I was no longer safe in the realms of childhood, till my hand was grabbed by a hot female hand, was snatched up too. I mean, my big plan for the evening was to throw on the bonfire, for a laugh, a German incendiary bomb that I had treasured for nearly five years. But the bomb bounced out of my coat pocket, and was never seen again. It probably wouldn't have gone off anyway . . .

Oh, how we danced! The firelight flickering on female faces laughing as if joy would never end, as if the world was reborn. Bare female arms flung around with abandon, female bosoms heaving under prewar frocks, worn to the thinness of tissue. I was flung from female to female, there was no jealousy that night, no competition, they were indeed a sisterhood. And the kissing. I have never, before or since, known such wild kissing. I think I must have kissed every woman in our village who had two legs to dance on.

'Can I borrow your lovely boy?'

'Here y'ar, love.' And I was in another set of warm, embracing female arms.

Flames streamed from the bonfire like great banners. Showers of sparks, like glowing flocks of birds, floated away over the dark of the harbour. The world of darkness and death was done away, the world they had followed their menfolk into so faithfully. Now, it was the women's hour, and anything wonderful might happen.

I noticed with some alarm, in a brief pause while the band got their breath back, that all three young soldiers had vanished . . . I was practically alone.

And then she came walking into the firelight, quite alone. Margie. Her hair washed and brushed and behind a ribbon, her dress new, or at least spotless and pretty. There was a little hush, a little pause that gave respect to death for the last time, and then the band struck up again, and she took me in her arms.

And we danced alone, while the women clapped and sang in time with the music. And death was done away. And finally, ribbon gone, hair flying, laughing, she danced me clean out of the circle and into the dark, and the last view I had of the female faces watching us, they were nodding and approving.

I will not tell you where we went, or what we did that night. It is a secret I shall carry to the grave. All I will say is that it did no harm to me, and no harm to her, though she did move down to Whitby soon afterwards, to marry a Whitby lad who was a very successful skipper. She is a grandmother now, God bless her.

Nobody ever mentioned that night to me. Not even my mother, let alone my father, when he came home from the fishing with a wonderful catch of fish. But I often think of it, how wonderful it was, the women's hour, and how swiftly it vanished into the hard uphill drag of austerity. I wonder whether, left to themselves, women would make the world quite different, given the chance. And even whether, back in the past, there were other women's hours, when bonfires blazed on every hilltop and headland, and women danced, and their men weren't so reluctant to join the dance with them. What a very different world that must have been.

The Authors

Sam McBratney won the Irish Book Trust Bisto Book of the Year Award for the best teenage novel of 1992 with *Put a Saddle on the Pig*. He writes: 'SWALK is all about timing. When I was about eleven or so I was confined to bed with a thing called scarlet fever. Two girls I knew found out where I lived and sent me home-made 'get well soon' cards with the four-letter word 'love' written on them, and they even came to my door to ask my mother how I was.

This was awful for me. It was worse than the scarlet fever. I was a sitting duck – and totally unable to do anything except wish they would go away and drown themselves.

'Some years later, when I yearned to be irresistible, I found that I seemed to have less magnetism than I'd had at eleven. What an awful thing it is when – like Monty in the story – you peak too soon.'

Vivien Alcock is the acclaimed author of, among other books, *The Monster Garden* and *The Trial of Anna Cotman*. She writes: 'For me, growing up was like climbing a slippery hill. I kept thinking I'd made it when, whoops, down I'd go to the bottom again, howling like a baby over a broken toy. I don't think I ever found a definite frontier between childhood and adulthood. Sometimes I'd take a giant step forward, like the day I decided I preferred boys to frogs. But it was never a steady preference. Even now, when I quarrel with my husband, I think wistfully of frogs.

'It's funny. I got a certificate for being born, for passing exams, for getting married, but nothing, not even the smallest scrap of paper, for becoming an adult. Perhaps, in spite of my age, I never quite made it.'

Jacqueline Wilson won the Federation of Children's Book Groups Award for *The Suitcase Kid*. She writes: 'I've written at least a dozen books about girls at the in-between stage. It's a time that's always fascinated me, because you feel so intensely at that age. I kept very long and self-absorbed diaries throughout my early teens (talk about Adrienne Mole!) and on one page I'd write about my passionate and co-existing loves for the boy on the bus, the smily man at the garage, the Polish teacher at school, my best friend's cousin and both Everly brothers, Don and Phil. The very next page I'd write enthusiastically about an elaborate imaginary game involving several sets of paper dolls. I'd step from the world of boys to the world of toys, barging backwards and forwards through that door to adulthood. I'm still not sure I'm always on the adult side of the door now, when I'm forty-something, not fourteen. Tiny toy animals trot across my desk as I type this, and the pictures stuck all over the wall above me portray wildly assorted pin-ups: my husband and daughter smile down at me, Virginia Woolf gazes into the middle distance, pink Picasso nudes nudge up against dainty medieval Madonnas, while Freddie Mercury prances up and down in his white vest.

'I suppose I literally slammed the door on my childhood when I left home at seventeen and went to live five hundred miles away in a girls' hostel in Scotland. I worked on a teenage magazine which was great fun and I made a lot of good friends, but I did feel very homesick at first. It was wonderful to go home that first Christmas – but I realised it wasn't really *my* home any more. I'd grown up and moved on.'

Rachel Anderson won the Guardian Children's Fiction Award for *Paper Faces*. She writes: 'The change from being a child to an adult can take about two seconds, or about fifty years. Sometimes I'm nearly there. I've been nearly there before, when I was seven, and when I was eleven. Also when I was fourteen and at nearly eighteen (although, in those days, you couldn't officially be an adult till twenty-one).

'Becoming a grown-up doesn't seem to happen all at once, or even once. It seems to be more of a long slow slide, with bumps in it.

'During growing up, one spends a lot of time thinking about oneself. So perhaps one part of becoming an adult is when one stops thinking only of oneself and sees things from the other person's point of view, which is what the self-absorbed boy does in his story about Roz. It doesn't make him any happier. But maybe it'll make him into a wiser person, or more likeable.'

Elizabeth Laird won the Federation of Children's Book Groups Award for *Kiss the Dust*. Her most recent book is *Hiding Out*. She writes: There is a moment when you know you have grown up. It has something to do with feeling powerful, and realising that you are in control.

'I think I was about fourteen when it happened

to me. I was looking in the mirror in the bathroom, brushing my hair back into a ponytail (they were fashionable then). I suddenly decided to take a train to London and go shopping on my own.

'I'm going out,' I told my mother, 'and I'll probably be late for supper.'

'I was amazed that she didn't ask me where I was going, or try to stop me.

'As I walked down the road to the station, I felt scared and gloriously free. I knew the rest of my life had begun.'

Joanna Carey is currently the Children's Books Editor of the *Guardian*. She is the author and illustrator of a number of books for younger children. She writes: 'My story was inspired by a girl I used to teach. She was uncommunicative at first, but the ice was broken when we began to talk about shoes. She always wore trainers – so did I – so did her mum. Even her grandad probably had a pair mouldering away under his bed. Before trainers were invented, when I was young, your shoes were a pretty good indication of not just your age but also how grown up you were – or thought you were. I spent my adolescent years in a repressive boarding school; in summer we wore beige socks and sandals and in winter thick liver-coloured stockings and hefty black lace-ups. Released at seventeen to go to art school I celebrated by buying some high-heeled purple suede T-strap shoes. Undeniably grown up, I sashayed into the Tate Gallery. Stepping back to contemplate a Matisse I got both heels firmly wedged in the iron grill of the underfloor ventilation system. It was embarrassing kneeling there, trying to wrench them out. A security guard helped. The shoes were ruined.

'The doorway to adulthood, like that to the Tate Gallery, is a revolving door; it ushers you in respectfully enough but, if you're not careful, if you push too hard, it whirls you round a couple of times and then leaves you right back where you started.'

Michael Morpurgo is the much acclaimed author of *War Horse, When the Whales Came, Waiting for Anya* and most recently *The War of Jenkins' Ear*. He writes: 'I suppose that growing from childhood to adulthood must be little more than a prolonged series of collisions, in my case so prolonged I fear I may never reach adulthood at all.

'I often look at my handwriting and think: you write just like you did when you were ten — unformed and unkempt. A grandfather of two, I look in the mirror in the mornings and consider myself. I must be a grandfather in the eyes of my grandchildren, but in my own I just can't be. I seem to have stuck somewhere between eight and eighteen.

'I was thinking about my reluctant maturity when considering Miriam's brief for a story, and wondered why my own series of collisions had done so little to make me grow up. I'd written several books on the subject, *Little Foxes, The War of Jenkins' Ear, Why the Whales Came, Mr Nobody's Eyes* — all of them chart these child/adult collisions and their results. But fiction is one thing, I'm another. Why have I never grown up *properly*? Perhaps, I thought, because my life has been too easy. I had a good upbringing. I have a comfortable home, a wonderful marriage, healthy children. Yes, my grandparents died, and my mother died only very recently. But in general the gods have spoken softly over me. Perhaps to grow up you have to suffer more, perhaps there has to be trauma. I don't know, but maybe there's some truth in that.

'I wanted to explore the effects of trauma on a child's life. How must it be to witness the horrors of adult violence? How must it be to lose everything, childhood, home, happiness at one stroke?

'This August I wandered the streets of Oradour in France (over six hundred villagers were massacred here in 1944). I thought of Marzabotto, Lidici, of Somalia, of Vietnam, of Bosnia. I thought of Sofia.'

Ian Strachan was shortlisted for the Whitbread Award for *The Flawed Glass*. His most recent novel is *The Boy in the Bubble*. He writes: 'At the time, my first girlfriend made me feel grown up. I also thought I grew up when I left home, at the age of sixteen, to go to college in London. I imagined smoking was very grown up, until I realised it was merely stupid. I thought I grew up at eighteen when I got my first job in the professional theatre. By the time I was twenty-five I believed I was getting close to being grown up when we acquired a house and a mortgage! But to my parents, I was still the feckless, irresponsible child I had always been. I deluded myself into believing I was good at relationships. It's only as I've got older that I've realised most of the relationships I've been in have survived far more because of other people's tolerance than from anything I did. Maybe that realisation *is* growing up. But then, there are always people, younger or older than ourselves, who can teach us important things and so perhaps we never are truly grown up. So, maybe we never are finally grown up and I'm still only on course for a giant leap between puberty and senility.'

Adèle Geras has recently completed the much praised Egerton Hall trilogy. She writes: 'When I was fourteen, I did spend the school summer holidays in The Gambia, where my father was working. It was during a dance at the club that someone kissed me properly for the very first time. I returned to England feeling as though I had news for all my friends: I could tell them about Jean from Alsace, with his pale turquoise eyes, and demonstrate how my French had improved through my association with him.

'I thought my romance was the most important thing in the world until I came upon my mother one day, comforting a good friend of hers (call her Joan, which was not her real name) who was weeping on our verandah. Poor Joan was mourning the loss of a lover whose very existence came as a dreadful shock to me. I knew her husband and son . . . could this really be happening outside a novel? At that moment, I understood with awful clarity the huge, tangled nets of pain that love can weave around people, and I felt completely grown up when I recognised that there was disappointment, disillusion and loss lying in wait for everyone who felt as I did when I was smooching in the back of Jean's 2CV.'

Alick Rowe was commended for the Carnegie Medal for *Voices of Danger*. His most recent novel is *The Panic Wall*. He writes: '*In Between* is a good title. When I look back to my teenage years I seem to have been in between just about everything. Mostly I was caught between home life in a working-class pub and making my way in a minor public school but I also suffered the in-betweenness of feeling I was an ordinary child burdened with adult responsibilities. Perhaps I should have written about those experiences but growing up in a small city in the fifties was such a dull experience that I didn't want to revisit it. The modern hero and the heroine of my story – *The Facts of Life* – are caught between school and parents, childhood and adulthood, friends and foes, even between different timetables. Growing up is a struggle between fantasy and reality so a human biology class seems to me a good setting. The only sex education my school provided was hidden away in nature study and all I can remember is studying the private parts of frogs – which, so far, has been of no great use to me.'

Robert Westall, who died in 1993, was one of the greatest writers of children's books; among the most famous are *The Machine Gunners*, *Blitz Cat* and *The Kingdom by the Sea*. His most recent novel, which deals superbly with the idea of being in between, is *Falling into Glory*.

In a letter in August 1992 he talked about the difference between being a child and an adult. 'I think young people should not be forced straight to adult tastes, but should be given a nibble of a little bit of this, and a little bit of that, so they can build their own menu.

'It carried me straight back to the feeling of being an unopened bud. I look back on my life and find it has not been unfruitful, but oh the excitement of being an unopened bud again! So much of me is outside me now, mined to make the books, that I do feel a bit like a half-worked-out coalmine.'